CLASSIC
MEXICAN
COOKING

CLASSIC MEXICAN COOKING

SALLY AND MARTIN STONE

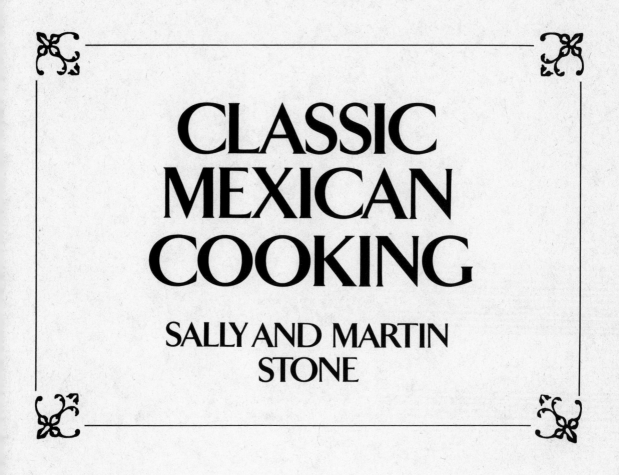

A WALLABY BOOK
PUBLISHED BY POCKET BOOKS NEW YORK

To our family and friends,
both North and South of the border:
Muchas gracias.

Another *Original* publication of WALLABY BOOKS

A Wallaby Book published by
POCKET BOOKS, a division of Simon & Schuster, Inc.
1230 Avenue of the Americas, New York, N.Y. 10020

ISBN: 0-671-50514-9

First Wallaby Books printing January, 1985

10 9 8 7 6 5 4 3 2 1

WALLABY and colophon are registered trademarks
of Simon & Schuster, Inc.

Printed in the U.S.A.

CONTENTS

INTRODUCTION

RECIPES

INTRODUCTION

DEBUNKING THE AMERICAN MYTH ABOUT MEXICAN FOOD

Mexican food in this country is about at the point where Italian food was fifty years ago, when most Americans thought of it as "that red stuff": it was all tomato sauce to them, served on overcooked, slimy spaghetti, and was thought to be too spicy and garlicky for the sensitive American palate. As recently as the late 1970s, several Mexican-American cookbooks proclaimed that Mexican food was based on chili peppers and beans. Their authors had the same preconceived ideas most Americans have about the Mexican kitchen.

Just as world travelers brought back the astounding news, after World War II, that Italian food came in other colors of the Italian flag—green, even white—Americans traveling to Mexico and culinary experts have begun to spread the word that Mexican food is not all refried beans and mouth-searing seasonings; Mexican food is not based solely on hot chilies any more than French Provençale cooking is based solely on garlic. Mexican food is not subtle, but it's not all hot by a long shot. One thing it does have is character. Mexican cuisine is a sophisticated, artful mix of Aztec, Spanish, French, Italian, and Austrian foods and techniques, combined with some unique indigenous ingredients—and is both delicious and varied. Chocolate, coffee, vanilla, sweet potatoes, pineapple, and scores of other foods on our daily shopping lists originated in Mexico. Mexican food can be, and is, more often than not, truly inspired.

Native Mexican food, especially as served in places tourists rarely frequent, is exciting and bears no relation to the fast food served at "Mexican" emporiums in the United States. At La Gorda ("The Fat One," a restaurant on a back street in Cuernavaca), for example, the Fat One herself will fish a huge potato from a bubbling caldron of oil, place it on a plate, smash it with the side of her calloused hand, sprinkle it generously with thick slices of boned and poached chicken breast, pour thin, fresh sour cream over it, and top it off with a large ladleful of salsa verde. The dish is simple, yet transports the diner to culinary paradise. So, while Mexican food can often seem exotic to the American taste, most Mexican food is not as much exotic as it is different or unknown.

While the vast majority of Americans think of Mexican cuisine as the fast food of roadside stands, most "authentic" Mexican cookbook authors in the United States offer Mexican recipes that are anything but fast; they take time, effort, and (preferably) several helpers. There are many dishes that require long cooking times, elaborate methods and techniques, and time-consuming preparation. Today, however, Mexican cooks want to be freed from the kitchen as quickly as possible—just like their American counterparts. Their interest in food has not waned; it's just that they have no time to waste. Their interests, like ours, extend far beyond the kitchen. We don't haul our own water, churn our own butter, or mill our own flour. We don't have to or want to. We use packaged goods that are as good as homemade and often better;

so do modern Mexicans. There is no reason to grind corn when Quaker Oats and others make a perfect *masa harina* for thickening or making tortillas or tamales.

Just as everything Mexican is not hot, every Mexican meal served doesn't take hours of preparation. Traditional methods have given way to modern, quick techniques; Mexican cooking has come of age. Mexican food preparation has always needed to be streamlined, and it is now being streamlined in millions of Mexican kitchens. Shortcut techniques and convenience foods have taken over south of the border along with the realization that judicious use of prepackaged foods can create traditional flavors in very little time. And new appliances are turning out textures even more pleasing to the contemporary palate than some of the traditional ones. In this book, we present the new, streamlined version of Mexican cooking, and are happy to report that nothing—not flavor, texture, or appeal—is lost in the transition.

MEXICAN COOKING IN THE AMERICAN KITCHEN

Authentic Mexican cooking is a truly remarkable cuisine—with many surprises. Once learned, it will become an important part of your culinary repertoire. You'll have gained mastery of an exciting, sometimes exotic, cuisine, perfect for everyday dining or for entertaining.

The recipes in this book explore the regional cuisines of Mexico as practiced in home kitchens of the middle and upper classes. Recipes have been adapted for the American kitchen, with as little variation as possible from the taste of the original recipes. To make the dishes in this book, you will need some basic equipment, a few culinary skills, and—to save time—a proper, up-to-date, and well-stocked larder.

INGREDIENTS

In many parts of the country, it is sometimes difficult when cooking Mexican foods to find the right fresh ingredients. They exist, of course, in parts of New York, Los Angeles, Chicago, and other big cities, and in the Southwest. But even there they are generally not available at the corner store. Fortunately, modern freezing and canning methods help, and many of the same ingredients Mexicans use at home can be mail-ordered and delivered right to your door. Most of the herbs and spices important to Mexican food can be found on supermarket shelves; others can be mail-ordered, or can be dispensed with completely when they add minimally to the flavor of a completed dish (fresh coriander, however, is indispensable, and is widely available at Mexican, Spanish, Cuban, Italian, and Oriental markets). Another way to get around the paucity of ingredients is through the careful use of substitutes (the chapter on Ingredients for Mexican Cooking includes information on many acceptable substitutes). Specific ingredients for Mexican cooking are listed in the next chapter.

EQUIPMENT

Most American kitchens today are equipped to produce authentic Mexican dishes. You probably have a blender and/or food processor, which is important; even a Mexican kitchen with two or three in help would be lost without a blender. In almost every case, whenever a recipe calls for preparation in a food processor, a blender may be used—and vice versa. The difference in texture obtained is minimal. Purists may wish to purée by pressing foods by hand or by using a *molcajete* (the Mexican mortar and pestle). However, when it comes to slicing, chopping, and mincing, there is nothing like a good sharp knife and a well-worn chopping board. These produce food pieces that are uniform in size, and their use requires minimal clean-up.

You probably have stainless-steel, aluminum, or enameled iron casseroles on your shelves. These can take the place of traditional Mexican earthenware casseroles and pots, although the hand-thrown, decorative Mexican cooking and serving dishes are inexpensive and a festive addition to the table. They also keep food hot longer. Make sure, if you decide to buy one, that you follow the instructions for seasoning it. You might also want to invest (minimal) in a tortilla press and a *comal* (a round iron or earthenware baking sheet—a griddle will do just as well).

INGREDIENTS FOR MEXICAN COOKING

What follows is a list of important ingredients used in Mexican cooking.

Achiote (or annatto): The little red seed of the annatto tree. Achiote seed is used extensively in Latin American cooking as a flavoring and coloring agent. In Mexico it is ground to a paste and sold in this form, but the paste is rarely seen in food stores in this country. To make achiote paste from the seeds found in the Latin American sections of most supermarkets and at Caribbean and Latin American food stores, first cover them with water and simmer for about 10 minutes; leave to soak for several hours (overnight is best); drain; crush the damp seeds in a mortar and then grind them as fine as possible in a blender or food processor.

Acitrón: Candied cactus. Available in

some supermarkets and Latin American groceries. Not to be confused with citron (too strong) or candied fruits. Substitute candied pineapple or sweet potato. *Acitrón* has little or no flavor. It is used for texture more than anything else. Don't fret if the recipe calls for it and you leave it out.

Avocados: Hard avocados should be allowed to mature in a warm place for at least 3 days. Ripe avocados should be tender to the touch—giving under a little finger pressure—but not soft. Shake an avocado—which should be the consistency of cream cheese—to be sure the pit hasn't left the flesh.

Avocado leaves: These add an elusive flavor and authenticity to some dishes. Toast them on a grill first, and use them either whole or ground, according to the recipe. (Use your blender to grind them.) Don't expect to find avocado leaves at your greengrocer's. Pluck a few leaves from a home-grown avocado plant. They won't be as strongly flavored as commercial leaves, but they'll do in a pinch.

Banana leaves: These are used for wrapping foods in little packages to be steamed (tamales) or to line baking pans for tamale pies. Banana leaves are pretty for presentation and are available in some Latin American markets. Aluminum foil, however, makes an efficient, if not aesthetic, substitute.

Chayotes: These are knobby, pear-shaped vegetables that belong to the gourd family. They are indigenous to Mexico and range from deep green to whitish in color. Those available in the United States are usually of the pale green variety, weigh about a pound, and are not heavy on flavor. You can use small fat zucchini where chayotes are called for, but do not precook them.

Cheese: Just as in other Western cuisines, cheese is used in Mexican cooking for color, flavor, and texture. The Indians learned to incorporate cheeses into their native dishes soon after the Spanish introduced dairy cattle, about 1530. Most recipes in this book call for a mild white cheese called *queso fresco,* which is often sold in markets that carry Mexican food. It is packaged in small, round shapes and can be sliced, crumbled, or shredded. You may substitute a mild feta, farmer cheese, or cheddar for crumbling; Monterey Jack, fresh mozzarella, or Muenster for slicing and melting; Parmesan (imported) for soups and gratinéed dishes; and a braided string cheese (without caraway seeds) for *quesadillas,* stuffing chilies, and for melting.

Chilies: (See the next chapter.)

Chocolate: Mexican chocolate is drinking chocolate, and is a mixture of chocolate, almonds, sugar, and cinnamon. It is packaged in bars with triangular sections. There is no substitute. For baking and other uses, follow the recipes and use the chocolate called for: unsweetened, semisweet, or cocoa powder.

Cinnamon: We like to use stick cinnamon, but ground cinnamon is fine for most recipes and even preferred in some.

Chorizo sausage: Spanish chorizos come canned and packed in lard, and are available in many markets. Mexican chorizos are fresh, and are coarser and softer. If neither is available, use a good Italian sausage. Do not substitute breakfast sausages.

Cooking fat and oil: Lard is the preferred fat for frying in traditional Mexican recipes. However, lard has a strong flavor and is not recommended because of its high cholesterol content. Use a good vegetable, peanut, or safflower oil instead. Butter is becoming more and more popular for cooking in Mexico, both for its flavor and delicacy.

Coriander (or cilantro): The ground dried seeds of this plant and its fresh green leaves are used extensively in Mexican cooking. There is no substitute. Do not use the leaves and ground seeds interchangeably; they have completely different tastes. Coriander seeds can always be found ground on your supermarket spice shelf.

The fresh coriander leaves, which look like flat Italian parsley, can be bought in bunches at all Latin American, Caribbean, Indian, and Oriental markets, and are becoming more and more popular with American greengrocers as well. Coriander leaves are often sold with roots intact. Don't remove them until you use the leaves; wrap the bunch in paper toweling, place it in a plastic storage bag, and store in the refrigerator. Don't rinse the leaves until you're ready to use them either, or they might rot. Refresh coriander leaves by sticking the roots in cold water for a few minutes. Coriander leaves can also be successfully frozen. Don't substitute parsley for the leaves, as it will give the recipe a completely different flavor.

Corn husks: Buy them in a Latin American market, or keep a store of your own, stripped from summer corn and dried in the sun or a very slow oven. Trim the leaves square on the ends, tie in bundles, and store in a dry place for future use.

Cream: Use fresh heavy cream, not the ultrapasteurized kind. When the recipe calls for sour cream, use crème fraîche, if you can get it or you can also make your own (according to the recipe below). If not, use a commercial brand thinned with a little milk. Use plain yogurt in a pinch, although it may be too sour a taste for some.

Homemade Sour Cream or *Crème fraîche*

1 cup heavy cream
1 or 2 tablespoons buttermilk

Combine cream and buttermilk in a jar; cover tightly and shake well. Let mixture sit near a pilot light (not on it) or in a warm place for 6 to 8 hours. Store in refrigerator. Keeps 4 to 6 weeks.

Epazote: This herb has a distinctive taste and is available dried in Latin American markets. It is also called *pazote* or Jerusalem oak. In this book, it is an optional ingredient.

Huitlacoche: This is a black fungus that forms on ears of corn. It has a deep mushroomy flavor, and is available canned in some Mexican markets.

Jícama: This is a brown-skinned root vegetable often found in Latin American and Oriental markets. The flesh is white, juicy, and crisp. It is eaten by the Mexicans as a snack or in salads. Street vendors sell thick slices of jícama peeled, salted, and sprinkled with lime juice and/or chili powder.

Herbs: Use dried herbs in these recipes unless fresh are specified. Herbs to have on hand are bay leaf, *epazote* (if available), oregano, and thyme.

Lettuce: Mexicans use romaine lettuce, which is widely available here. Iceberg is a good substitute when crunch and color are needed.

Masa harina: Handmade tortillas are the best tortillas and are fashioned from fresh *masa*, tortilla dough made by soaking and cooking dried corn kernels in a mixture of unslaked lime and water to remove the husks; the softened corn is then ground to a smooth paste. *Masa harina* made by the Quaker Oats Company is widely available and is produced in the traditional manner especially for making tortillas. The term *masa* is used in Mexico to refer to both the dough and the flour. In this book, it is used to refer to the flour.

Mexican green tomatoes or **Tomates Verdes:** These are not tomatoes at all (they are not green, or unripe, red tomatoes). *Tomates verdes* are covered with a thin papery husk, are the size of apricots, and are a grayish green in color. Available fresh in Latin American markets and canned in the Latin American section of most supermarkets, Mexican green tomatoes are usually called *tomatillos*, or sometimes "peeled green tomatoes." To prepare fresh Mexican green tomatoes, remove husks, rinse, and just cover with water. Bring water to a boil and lower to

13

a simmer for 10 minutes. Drain and process *tomatillos* to a smooth sauce using a little of the cooking water. Cooked *tomatillos* freeze well.

Nopal cactus: The joints and pads of the prickly pear cactus are available fresh in some markets, but the canned (in water or vinegar) are fine for recipes in this book. Cut into small pieces (about ½ inch) they are called *nopalitos*. To cook fresh nopal cactus, trim the sharp spines or thorns around the edges, cut into strips or dice small, and simmer in salted water to cover for about 10 minutes, or until tender; place in a colander and rinse under cold water to remove the sap released in the cooking.

Piloncillo: Unrefined sugar that's molded into little cone shapes. Use dark brown sugar instead.

Plantains: Available in all Spanish markets, plantains are similar to bananas in taste and appearance but firmer in texture. Choose fruit that is black-skinned and soft to the touch. Firm green bananas may be substituted.

Pumpkin seeds (or pepitas): These are available in Mexican and Latin American markets and health food stores, hulled, untoasted, and unsalted. Store in a cool, dry place; they keep indefinitely. The ground seeds have been used as a base for sauces and as a thickening agent since before Cortés.

Sesame seeds: Introduced by the Spanish (who in turn were introduced to them by the Moors) sesame seeds are used throughout Mexico in sauces such as *mole poblano* and *pipián*. Buy them loose—the white seeds only—in health food and specialty stores, or in jars at the supermarket. They may also be purchased toasted, but are often costly that way. It's easy to do yourself. Place seeds in a dry skillet over a medium flame and stir constantly, so they don't burn, until seeds are a lovely golden color. Store in a cool, dry place, tightly covered; they will keep indefinitely.

Seville oranges: Sour oranges. Not easy to come by in the United States. If they are not sold in your area, substitute fresh orange juice with a little lemon juice added.

Shrimp, dried: You'll find these, cleaned, and with heads and tails removed, in most Oriental grocery stores and Latin American markets. They are used in Mexico for their flavor and are not eaten alone.

Squash blossoms: These are hard to find here but are sold at some Italian markets. They are very fragile and don't keep very long once picked. If you have a garden, pick most of the male blossoms (leaving a few to ensure regeneration). The female blossoms have a miniature squash in the center of the flower and will continue to produce. Pumpkin, zucchini, and squash blossoms are interchangeable for cooking purposes.

Tomatoes: Fresh tomatoes are usually specified in this book, but please use the canned Italian tomatoes during the many months of the year when only cardboard "slicing tomatoes" are available. Canned tomatoes should be drained and used cup for cup for fresh tomatoes.

Tortillas: The fresh kind are always preferable, but the frozen ones available in supermarkets everywhere are quite acceptable (making them yourself is time-consuming and chancey until you perfect the method, so use the frozen or fresh from a Mexican market if there is one nearby). The canned variety are generally not as good.

Vinegar: Many Mexican recipes call for vinegar. This is a mild, white vinegar. You may use Japanese rice vinegar or a good red wine vinegar if you like.

If you plan on cooking Mexican, you should probably add the following ingredients to what you already have in your kitchen or pantry.

Beans: 2 pounds of your choice of dried beans: black, kidney, California pink, speckled

1 large can refried beans (for when time is a problem)

Dried chilies: At least ½ pound each of *chiles anchos, cascabel, mulatos,* and *pasillas* (all keep well in sealed packages or tightly covered jars)

Green chilies (or poblanos): 2 cans (4 ounces each) chopped

2 cans (4 ounces each) peeled, cut in strips

2 cans (7 ounces each) peeled, whole

2 cans (27 ounces each) peeled, whole

Chiles serranos: 2 small cans en *escabeche*

Chiles jalapeños: 3 small cans en *escabeche*

Chiles chipotles: 1 small can en *vinagre*

Flour and Rice: 1 bag (5 pounds) of Quaker *masa harina*

1 box (2 pounds) of long-grain rice

Herbs:
Dried bay leaves
Epazote (Jerusalem oak, *pazote*)
Marjoram
Oregano
Thyme
Mint
Saffron
Parsley

Mexican green tomatoes: 4 small cans (10 ounces each)

Nuts and seeds: ½ pound each of almonds (whole or slivered), pecans, peanuts (unsalted), walnuts, sesame seeds (white, untoasted), pumpkin seeds (*pepitas,* hulled, unsalted), pine nuts or unroasted cashews (the pieces are fine and less expensive). (*Note:* Nuts and seeds, ground very fine, are used for thickening sauces in Mexican kitchens rather than the flour, eggs, and cream of European cooking. You can easily pulverize nuts and seeds in a blender or food processor. Sometimes *masa harina* is used instead, especially by the more inventive "new" cooks.)

Oil and vinegar: ½ gallon peanut oil
½ gallon corn or safflower oil
1 bottle (10 ounces) of Japanese rice vinegar
1 quart mild white or red wine vinegar

Spices: A small-size box or can each of achiote, allspice, aniseed, stick cinnamon, whole cloves, coriander (whole seeds and/or ground), cumin (whole or ground), pepper (whole corns), vanilla (bean and/or vanilla extract).

Tomatoes: 4 large cans (35 ounces each) of Italian peeled tomatoes (whole, not puréed)

4 small cans (10 ounces each) of tomatoes with green chilies

Miscellaneous: 1 bottle of capers (the large size, in vinegar)
1 small can of nopal cactus, *nopalitos*
1 or 2 jars or cans of pitted green olives
1 large bar of Mexican chocolate
1 large jar of Knorr Mexican chicken bouillon powder (*caldo de pollo*)

You might also like to have on hand a box of raisins, a small quantity of dried shrimp, corn husks you've dried and saved from the summer crop, a large can of white hominy, a box of kosher salt, several fresh heads of garlic, 5 pounds of good yellow or white onions, a few red onions, a few pounds of all-purpose potatoes, and—but *only* if you use it often enough—a bunch of fresh coriander (otherwise buy only as you need it because it keeps, at best, less than 2 weeks).

In the freezer you might keep a supply of frozen tortillas (both corn and wheat), buttermilk (in ½ cup containers); in the refrigerator, a pint of sour cream, homemade *crème fraîche,* heavy cream, mild cheddar, Monterey Jack, and Parmesan cheeses.

CHILIES

Chili-seasoned "hot" foods have been consumed by humans for more than eight thousand years. Long before the Greeks and Romans used pepper as legal tender, the Mexican and South American Indians were eating incendiary wild chilies.

Botanically, chilies are *capsicums* (family: *Solanaceae*) or red peppers. There are two varieties: the large "sweet" type or bell, and the smaller chili. Bell peppers are used as vegetables, raw or cooked. Chilies, on the other hand, are used as condiments, flavorings, or pickles, or are powdered and used as spices. Some say there are forty varieties of chilies, some say sixty-one, some ninety-two, and others over a hundred. We will be concerned with only a tiny fraction of the scores cultivated. And even these few can be narrowed down.

Unfortunately, the names of chilies vary depending on where you are. It's easy to get confused, but the names don't really seem to matter. Chilies cross-fertilize so that even within a species there are variations. What this is leading up to is a little practical advice: Don't buy chilies by name; buy them by color, size, and appearance.

DRIED CHILIES

The *ancho*, the most popular of the dried red chilies, is fairly large and is not terribly hot. It is, in fact, rather mild, but full of flavor. The *ancho* is the dried version of the *chile poblano*, and varies in size from 2 to 5 inches long and 1 to 3 inches wide. It is wrinkled and dark reddish-brown when you buy it and turns barn red when soaked.

The *mulato* is darker and browner than the *ancho*, and is longer and slightly more tapering in shape, with a more pungent flavor.

The *pasilla* is a long chili that is thin, brownish black in color, about 6 or 7 inches in length and 1 inch wide, and quite hot (or *picante*).

The *chipotle* is brick red (when you try to distinguish between brick and barn red, you realize that choosing chilies can be an art as exacting as choosing wine). It is wrinkled, smaller than the *ancho* and *mulato*, and has a smoky smell and an individual flavor. The *chipotle* is extremely *picante*. *Chipotles* are ripened, dried smoked *jalapeños*.

The *pequin* (or *tepin*) is tiny, red, and fiery.

PREPARING DRIED CHILIES

Most recipes require that dried chilies be soaked until soft and then puréed. To soften, simply place as many as you'll need, broken into pieces, in a saucepan with water to cover. Bring water to a boil. Remove from heat and allow the chilies to soften as they cool. Remove the veins, stems, and seeds. Place the tender flesh in a blender or a food processor with enough liquid to make a smooth paste. If any bits of seeds and skin remain, you can press the chilies through a sieve. (A little care in preparation can save this step.)

FRESH CHILIES

The *serrano* is tapered, green, and about 1½ inches long. It is quite hot. You'll not find it fresh too often; it is usually canned *en escabeche* (pickled with onions, carrots, and herbs).

The *jalapeño* has become the most visible of Mexican chilies. It is, of course, the most ubiquitous chili on the Mexican table. In the United States, little bits of *jalapeño* are mixed into a variety of cheeses, and *jalapeño* is often the only hot chili available in Mexican fast food establishments or canned in the Mexican food section of supermarkets. *Jalapeños* can be found fresh most of the time in California, the Southwest, Chicago, New York, and Florida. "Mild," pickled whole *jalapeños* in cans are fairly tame, but retain their flavor. They are about 2½ inches long by 1 inch wide.

The *poblano* is about the size of a bell pepper and is, most of the time, almost as mild. *Poblanos* can be hot, however. Their flavor is so distinctive that bell peppers should not be substituted unless fresh or canned *poblanos* are unavailable. Better yet, try substituting canned, peeled green chilies by Ortega (for stuffing), or fresh *chilies Anaheim* (California chilies, as the name implies). The Anaheim is available fresh in most markets; canned Anaheim chilies are available in the Tex-Mex section of supermarkets. The fresh Anaheim or California pepper should not be confused with green bell peppers. They are light green in color and have an elongated shape.

TO MAKE CHILIES LESS FIERY

Always remove the skin, stem, seeds, and veins from fresh chilies, that is where, it is said, most of the fire resides. Then soak the chilies in salted cold water or acidulated water (1 tablespoon vinegar to 2 cups water) for an hour or more (if the chili is especially hot). Then rinse.

PREPARING FRESH CHILIES

Before chilies or any kind of peppers can be peeled, their skins must be loosened by broiling, toasting, or grilling.

Broiling: Set broiler on high; place chilies on a foil-lined broiling pan or baking sheet 4 inches from the source of heat. Turn frequently with kitchen tongs until chilies are charred and blistered on all sides. Remove chilies and put them in a closed plastic or brown paper bag to "steam" for 10 to 15 minutes. When cool enough to handle, strip off the skin with your fingers (see note of caution below) or a knife.

Toasting or grilling: Set a wire rack over the stove burner (we use a handled, flat wire grater saved just for toasting chilies, green and red peppers, and eggplant) and set the heat to medium. Toast until charred and blistered all over, turning often with fork or tongs. (Or, impale one chili at a time on a long fork and hold it over the heat, turning to blister and char all sides.) Put the chilies in a plastic bag or brown paper bag, twist closed, and let them "steam" for 10 to 15 minutes before peeling.

NOTE OF CAUTION: Do not touch your eyes, face, or sensitive areas of your skin after handling chilies. Always wash your hands with soap and water. Be especially careful to scrape or brush under your fingernails, where tiny bits of pepper or cap-saicin oil can hide and wreak havoc later. Capsaicin won't do permanent damage, but its sting can be excru-ciatingly painful to eyes, lips, and the groin area. If you are especially sensitive, wear rubber gloves when han-dling chilies and wash again anyway.

FREEZING CHILIES

Chilies can be frozen successfully either peeled or blistered but unpeeled (they're easy to peel when thawed). It's best to freeze them one or two at a time so that you can thaw only the amount you will be using. To freeze, just wrap each chili in plastic wrap, put in plastic food storage bags, and freeze. Just reach into the bags and take out as many chilies as you need for a par-ticular recipe. Be sure to label as to type.

CANNED CHILIES

Fresh chilies are often difficult, if not impossible, to track down in many parts of the United States. Use canned chilies instead. Canned chilies come packed in brine, vinegar, oil (sometimes with other vegetables added), or sauce. They also come pickled (en escabeche). Check the recipe and read the label. You can't go too far wrong if you begin by using chilies sparingly. If a recipe calls for chiles serranos and your local Hispanic store or super-market has only canned jalapeños, chances are it will not ruin a dish.

When making chiles rellenos, you need firm green (California, Anaheim, or guero) chilies that will not disintegrate when stuffed or cooked in sauce. There are some whole green chilies that will do in a pinch, but be gentle in handling them—and experiment with different brands.

POWDERED CHILIES

Chili in powdered form is available from some markets. Chili powders are popular in Mexico, and their flavor is more than adequate.

HOW TO USE GROUND CHILIES

1 tablespoon ground equals 1 whole dried chile ancho, mulato, or pasilla; ⅛ teaspoon cayenne pepper equals 1 chile pequin.

Commercially packaged chili powders with added spices are different from powdered chilies. We do not recommend them as an adequate substi-tute—use them only in a pinch.

EATING CHILIES

Because of the heat chilies can generate in your mouth and on other sen-sitive tissues of the body, you'd expect them to have damaging effects on your digestive tract. But unless you are already suffering from gastrointes-tinal diseases, chilies, and their heat generating agent, capsaicin, are not going to harm you.

If you overdose and burn your mouth, try eating rice or bread or other ab-sorbent foods. Don't drink cold liquids; they only tend to spread the of-fending element to other parts of your mouth.

SOURCES FOR MEXICAN INGREDIENTS

Besides the stores listed below in alphabetical order according to city, many supermarkets, farmers' markets, specialty stores, and "gourmet" sections of large department stores carry ingredients needed to cook Mexican. If you discover that none of the places listed here are nearby or you dislike ordering by mail, try consulting the Yellow Pages for "Food Products—Mfrs. & Distrs.," "Gourmet Shops," or "Grocers—Whol." Call one and ask if they distribute Mexican foods and to whom. If they don't, ask if they know of another distributor or wholesaler in the area who might. Then try again.

ALBUQUERQUE

Valley Distributing Co.
2819 2nd St. N.W.
Albuquerque, NM 87107
  Retail and mail order.

ATLANTA

Rinconcito Latino
Ansley Square Mall
1492B Piedmont Ave. N.E.
Atlanta, GA 30309
  Retail.

BOSTON & Environs

Garcia Superette
397 Centre Ave.
Jamaica Plain
Boston, MA 02130
  Retail and mail order.

Star Market
625 Mt. Auburn St.
Cambridge, MA 02238
  Retail.

Stop and Shop
390 D St.
East Boston, MA 02228
  Retail.

CALIFORNIA

Many cities and towns have supermarkets that carry a variety of Mexican ingredients, due to the popularity of Tex-Mex cooking and the large Mexican population.

CHICAGO

La Casa del Pueblo
1810 Blue Island
Chicago, IL 60608
  Retail.

Casa Esterio
2719 West Division
Chicago, IL 60622
  Retail.

Casa Cardenas
324 South Halstead
Chicago, IL 60606
  Retail. Large variety.

Gourmet shops and departments of specialty stores in Chicago and its suburbs carry some Mexican ingredients, fresh, frozen, and canned.

DENVER

Safeway Supermarket
2660 Federal Blvd.
Denver, CO 80219
  Retail.

Casa Herrera
2049 Larimer St.
Denver, CO 80205
  Retail.

Johnnie's Market
2030 Larimer St.
Denver, CO 80205
  Retail.

El Progreso
2282 Broadway
Denver, CO 80205
  Retail.

DETROIT

The Mexican population in Detroit shops at several supermarkets in the Bagley area near the Windsor Bridge.

HOUSTON

There are many small Mexican grocery stores in Houston. The Rice and Weingarten supermarket chain carries some fresh ingredients, and canned or frozen ones.

LOS ANGELES

Most supermarkets in Los Angeles have a Mexican section. If you prefer, there is El Mercado in East Los Angeles, which is as close as you can come to a Mexican open market in the States. Or try the Central and Farmers' Markets.

NEW YORK CITY & Environs

There are innumerable Mexican, Latin American, Indian, and Oriental markets in all five boroughs where fresh, canned, dried, and frozen products may be obtained. Altman's, Bloomingdale's, Macy's, and other department stores in Manhattan and the suburbs (in New Jersey and Connecticut as well) plus nationally known gourmet shops such as Zabar's, Dean & DeLuca, H. Roth & Son, and others stock Mexican canned, frozen, and dried foods—and often fresh chilies and other produce as well. Most offer mail order catalogs. Then, of course, there is always the Latin American market under the railroad tracks on upper Park Avenue, where green chilies and coriander can be found all year around. Korean produce markets all over the city have green chilies and fresh coriander available whenever you need them. Supermarkets always seem to have a Mexican, Latin, or Tex-Mex section with American-packaged Mexican canned and dried goods. The most extensive selection of all can be found at Casa Moneo, that Mexican gastronomic haven on West 14th Street, just west of 7th Avenue. They also have a large variety of Mexican housewares, cooking equipment, serving pieces, and spices.

Casa Moneo
210 West 14th St.
New York, NY 10014
  Retail and mail order.

ST. LOUIS

Soulard Market
730 Carrol St.
St. Louis, MO
  Retail and mail order.

SAN DIEGO

Why not just hop in the car and go across the border to nearby Tijuana, where you can buy anything you need to cook Mexican?

SANTA FE

Theo. Roybal
Rear 212-216 Galisteo St.
Santa Fe, NM 87501
  Retail and mail order.

TEXAS

Because Mexican ingredients are part of the regional cooking of Texas, it is not difficult to find fresh and canned ingredients in local supermarkets and specialty food stores all over the state.

WASHINGTON, D.C.

La Sevillana
2469 18th St. N.W.
Washington, D.C. 20009
  Retail and mail order.

Casa Peña
1636 17th St. N.W.
Washington, D.C. 20009
  Retail and mail order.

Safeway International
1110 F St. N.W.
Washington, D.C. 20004
  Retail and mail order.

What in the World
5441 MacArthur Blvd. N.W.
Washington, D.C. 20016
  Retail and mail order.

Many specialty food stores in the city and its suburbs stock Mexican ingredients. Also try Williams-

Sonoma in Georgetown for cooking utensils and some simple ingredients (write for their catalog at the home base in San Francisco: Williams-Sonoma, Mail Order Department, P.O. Box 7456, San Francisco, CA 94120-7456). Retail and mail order.

HOW THE MEXICANS EAT

Desayuno begins the Mexican day. It's a breakfast, usually of sweet rolls or breads and *café con leche* (the Mexican equivalent of French *café au lait*). The alternate to coffee is hot chocolate. At about eleven or eleven-thirty in the morning, it's time for *almuerzo*, the Mexican version of our coffee break. *Almuerzo* is like an early lunch or brunch, and might include fruit or fruit juices, eggs, beans, tortillas, chili sauce, and *café con leche*.

Comida is the main meal of the day and is taken anytime from two p.m. to late afternoon. It's a heavy meal and might begin with soup, followed by a *sopa seca* (a rice or pasta course). Then a main course of meat, poultry, or fish is served, followed by a little green salad or a green vegetable dish. After this come beans, tortillas, and *bolillos* (rolls), with wine or beer to drink. Fresh or stewed fruit finish off the meal. Elaborate desserts are usually reserved for visitors or the special Sunday meal.

In the evening—nine or later—Mexicans take a light meal, consisting of a snack of sweet rolls, *atole* (a corn drink), coffee, chocolate, tacos, a little sandwich, some ham, perhaps a *sopa seca*; nothing too filling.

Cena, dinner, is served when there are guests to entertain or an occasion to celebrate. It's a late meal and is often a feast.

PUTTING TOGETHER A MEXICAN MENU

It's not difficult to put together a Mexican meal. Do it the way you plan an American meal: think about color and texture and don't use a major ingredient in more than one course.

There are many *moles, tingas,* and *sopa secas* that can be served as a one-dish meal with the addition of a salad course and dessert. A more elaborate meal might start with a "wet" soup or an *antojito* like *seviche,* followed by a simple chicken dish such as Chicken in Pumpkin Seed Sauce or Chicken on a Pounded Potato served with a tossed green salad and, perhaps, a pudding such as Chilled Mango Dessert to top it off. Lunch could consist of Asparagus in Almond Sauce with a few thin slices of boiled ham or smoked turkey. A wedge of Mexican Chocolate Cake washed down with *café de olla* would round out this elegant luncheon menu.

Sopa secas make wonderful first courses or luncheon main dishes. They're also perfect for a light supper with a salad accompanying them.

Remember that many Mexican entrées come complete with salad—shredded lettuce, chopped tomatoes, radishes, and onions. The sauces, especially *salsa cruda,* can also stand in for a salad or vegetable course.

To be typically Mexican, soup, *sopa seca,* vegetables, meat, fish or fowl, and salad would each be served as a separate course.

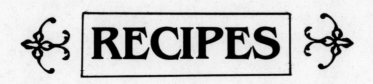

RECIPES

SOME BASICS: TORTILLAS, TAMALES, AND SAUCES

If you've been to Mexico, or eaten in a Mexican restaurant, you are probably familiar with words like *tortilla, tamale, enchilada,* and *taco,* and have probably tasted some of the many sauces that grace the Mexican table. In this chapter, you'll find many of the often-confusing terms—defined and explained. You'll also find recipes for some Mexican staples—tortilla and tamale dough, guacamole, *salsa verde.* Many of these basics are called for in other recipes.

TORTILLAS

Quite simply, tortillas are round, thin sheets of unleavened dough made from corn (in southern Mexico) or wheat (in the north). They are called "the bread of Mexico," but tortillas are also the pasta of Mexico and the crêpe of Mexico.

Nobody seems able to pinpoint when tortillas first appeared in Central America. But a good guess would be that tortillas first appeared after the domestication of maize (native corn), which probably coincided with the evolvement of farming societies.

Maize was, and still is, prepared by soaking the dried kernels overnight, or boiling them with unslaked lime and leaving them to soften. They are often ground to an even, uniform dough called *masa.* To make tortillas, the *masa* is flattened into round, thin cakes by hand or—more often, today—in a metal press. They are then toasted on an ungreased griddle, the *comal.* A coarser dough is used to make tamales.

Tortillas themselves don't have much flavor—they acquire texture and character from the other foods with which they are served. Fresh tortillas are "the spoons you can eat," used to transfer hundreds of Mexican dishes from plate to mouth. For this purpose they are usually cut into triangles and fried until they are crisp. In this guise, Mexicans call tortillas *totopos* or *tostaditas.* When not imitating a spoon or fork, tortillas often become plates; all kinds of sauces, bits of meat, vegetables, and cheese are piled on the "dishes," and they are eaten like a Danish open-faced sandwich or folded and eaten out of the hand. They can also be rolled and fried. These tortillas are called *tacos.*

When tortillas are cut into strips and fried, then tossed into a casserole and baked with meats, vegetables, cheese, and other ingredients, you have the Mexican *sopas secas* or "dry soups." In addition, fried tortilla strips thicken and add texture and flavor to soups. They can also be cut into pieces, dipped in sauce, fried, and topped with a myriad of sauces and other ingredients to become *chilaquiles.*

Stale and dried-out tortillas are ground up and formed into little dough balls—*gordas* or *bollitos*—and become Mexican dumplings.

Tostadas are whole tortillas fried flat like crisp pancakes and spread with refried beans, meat or chicken pieces, sauce, and fresh salad vegetables.

Wheat tortillas are used to make *burritos*.

As you can see, tortillas can be rolled, wrapped, fried, baked, filled, garnished, smothered, seasoned, ground, chopped, sliced, broken, boiled, or what have you; they are so versatile they can impersonate a spoon, a scoop, a fork, a plate, a sandwich, pasta, dumplings, noodles, crêpes, bread, croutons, pizza, pita, wontons, kreplach, blintzes, ravioli, and on and on.

How to Make Tortillas: If you can't buy tortillas fresh, buy them frozen. If the frozen are not available, acquire a tortilla press, some plastic sandwich bags, and make your own.

CORN TORTILLAS

1 cup Quaker *masa harina*
½ cup (a little more if necessary) cold water

1. Place the *masa harina* in a bowl and add the water all at once. Mix quickly with your fingers to make a soft dough. If the dough is too dry or crumbles, add a little more water. Set the dough aside for about 20 minutes, covered with a damp cloth.

2. Set an ungreased griddle or heavy-bottomed skillet over medium heat.

3. Cut down two closed sides of a plastic sandwich bag so that it opens like a book. Line a tortilla press with the bag so that the "spine" of the book coincides with the hinge of the press (in other words, the cut sandwich bag and the tortilla press should both open the same way). Form 6 or 8 balls of dough by dividing the dough equally. Flatten each ball and place one on the press a little toward the hinge rather than dead center. Close the press, firmly pushing down on the handle. Open the press and peel the plastic from the dough (not the other way around). If the dough sticks to the plastic, it is too wet. Put all the dough back into the bowl and work about 1 teaspoon of *masa harina* into it (more, if necessary). Divide and try again. If the dough is too dry, the pressed tortilla will crumble. Put it and the other pieces of dough back in the bowl and combine with about 1 teaspoon or more of water. Once you've got the right consistency, the plastic will peel from the tortillas without problems.

4. Now lay the tortilla carefully onto the hot griddle so that no air bubbles form. Cook until lightly flecked with brown, then turn and cook the other side. The whole thing should take no more than 2 minutes. As tortillas finish cooking, stack them and cover them with a dry towel or cloth napkin. The tortillas may seem a little stiff when you remove them from the griddle, but they will soften as they stand under the cloth. If you work slowly, the uncooked dough may dry out and you will have to add another tiny bit of water; keeping the uncooked dough balls covered with a damp cloth should preclude this step.

CAUTION: Cornmeal and *masa harina* are not interchangeable. Don't attempt tortillas with the cornmeal you're used to.

NOTE: If you don't own a tortilla press (metal or wooden), use a heavy flat-bottomed skillet to press out the dough between two layers of plastic wrap.

This recipe may be doubled, but do not attempt to triple or quadruple the amount. Start again with a new batch of dough, otherwise the raw dough will dry out before it is used up.

Makes 6–8 tortillas 5–6 inches in diameter

WHEAT OR FLOUR TORTILLAS

2 cups all-purpose flour
½ teaspoon salt
¼ cup solid shortening (Mexicans use lard)
½ cup tepid water (approximately)
More shortening (oil is okay)

1. Place flour and salt in a bowl; combine briefly. With your fingers, work in the solid shortening until it is mixed through evenly. While stirring, add enough water to make a soft dough. Divide the dough into 12 or 18 equal pieces and roll each piece into a round ball.
2. Coat each of the balls with oil and allow them to stand for about 15 minutes.
3. Set an ungreased griddle or large thick-bottomed skillet over medium heat.
4. With your palm, press each ball into a flat, round cake and sprinkle both sides with flour. Roll out each cake of dough on a lightly floured surface to an 8-inch round (for 12 tortillas) or a 6-inch round (for 18 tortillas).
5. Lay one tortilla on the preheated griddle and cook until bubbles form on the top side and the bottom is flecked with brown. Flip the tortilla, pressing down on the bubbles with a spatula, and cook until the second side begins to color. Cook the remaining tortillas, stacking them as they are done under a dry cloth or napkin. You may use them immediately or wrap them in foil and reheat them in a 400°F oven for a few minutes.

NOTE: Store-bought flour tortillas are perfectly acceptable. They are available (not everywhere in every size) in 4-, 6-, 8-, 12-, and 15-inch sizes. If you buy them frozen, thaw them, wrap them in foil, and heat them in a 350°F oven for 15 minutes.

Makes twelve 8-inch, or eighteen 6-inch tortillas

PUFFY WHEAT TORTILLAS

Packaged or homemade wheat tortillas 6 inches in diameter
Corn oil for deep frying

Pour 1 inch of oil into a 10-inch skillet. Heat to smoking. With tongs, gently place one tortilla in the oil and fry until puffy, crisp, and golden brown in spots. Remove with tongs and drain on paper towels. Repeat with each tortilla. Keep warm in the oven until serving time, or reheat (foil-wrapped) at 400°F for 5 minutes. These tortillas have an unusual, nutty taste. Serve instead of bread with any hot main dish.

Allow 1 or 2 tortillas per serving

Making and Filling Taco Shells: Tacos are grilled, filled tortillas. In Mexico they are served as snacks. They are served flat, folded, or filled, rolled and fried. In most cases, we suggest folding tacos American-style.

Corn tortillas
½ cup corn oil
Filling and garnishes of your choice

AMERICAN STYLE:
   1. Heat oil in a large skillet. Hold a flat corn tortilla of any size with tongs and dip both sides in the hot oil to soften; fold in half and fry both sides until crisp, turning once. Repeat until all are cooked. Drain, folded, on paper towels.
   2. To fill, pull sides apart gently so the tortilla does not break. Spoon in quantities of meat, beans, chicken, and sauce, and garnish with onions, scallions, lettuce, and/or chopped or sliced tomatoes. (See p. 42 for other taco fillings.)

MEXICAN STYLE:
   1. Soften tortillas before filling on a griddle, or wrap a quantity in foil and heat in a preheated 350°F oven for 15 minutes.
   2. Spoon some filling on each of the warmed tortillas; roll up and secure with a toothpick.
   3. Fry a few filled tortillas at a time in ¼ inch of oil until bottoms are golden; remove toothpick, turning as you do so, and fry, seam side down, until they are almost crisp. Drain on paper towels; open carefully and garnish with additional fillings, sauces, or cream, or serve with garnishes.

NOTE: You can buy preshaped taco shells in the supermarket. They'll do in a pinch. Just wrap them in foil and place in a preheated 350°F oven for about 15 minutes to soften before filling or frying.

Allow 2 tacos per serving

Making and Filling Enchiladas: Enchiladas are corn tortillas filled, rolled, covered with a sauce, and usually baked, then served with a choice of garnishes. (Some enchiladas are simply fried in hot oil for a few seconds on each side, filled, placed on a warm platter seam side down, covered with sauces and garnishes, and served.)
   Both filling and sauce are prepared in advance. Once enchiladas are filled, *do not* cover them with sauce unless you are going to bake them immediately—they turn mushy when allowed to sit in sauce.

Corn tortillas
Corn oil
Filling of your choice
Sauce (or cheese) of your choice

1. Soften tortillas by dipping them in hot oil one at a time. Turn with tongs, giving them only a few seconds on each side—just long enough to make sure the tortillas will not break or crack when you roll them. Drain briefly on paper towels.

2. Spread a spoonful of filling toward the bottom edge of each tortilla; roll up tightly and place, seam side down, in an ungreased baking dish spread with a thin coating of the sauce you are using (this will prevent sticking). When all the enchiladas are side by side in the dish, pour the sauce and/or cheese you are using over them and bake as directed.

NOTE: Any leftovers can be frozen; wrap in foil and freeze. When ready to serve, thaw for 2 hours or more and reheat at 350°F for 20 minutes or so.

TO PREPARE AHEAD: Fill and roll enchiladas, then spread their tops and edges with a tiny bit of sauce to keep them moist until they are put in the oven. Cover and refrigerate. Remove from refrigerator about 30 minutes before baking. Pour sauce over the enchiladas and sprinkle with cheese just before putting in a preheated 350°F oven.

Allow 2 enchiladas per serving for a main dish;
1 for an appetizer

TAMALES

Served in Mexico for a special occasion—a fiesta—tamales are probably more ancient than tortillas, which had to await the invention of the *metate* (or grinder) and the griddle before they could be made. Originally, tamale dough was simply wrapped in the tough, sturdy husks of corn, and the resulting package buried in the hot ashes of a fire. The husks protected the dough from the heat long enough for it to be cooked through—no cooking utensils needed! Once pottery was developed, the Indians started to steam tamales in underground pits or in covered pots in which a primitive trivet, corncobs, or stones were used to hold the tamales over an inch or so of boiling water.

The first tamales were probably plain; if they had any flavor at all it was absorbed from the corn husks. Eventually, however, the piquant chilies were used to spice up the bland dough. Modern tamales do not differ appreciably from those eaten thousands of years ago.

Tamales may contain nothing more than veins of chili, but, more than likely, they will have bits of chicken, beans, meat, fish, turkey, or any leftovers or scraps of food the cook has at his or her fingertips. There are sweet tamales (not a new invention, since the Aztecs sweetened them with honey). Tamales can range in size from 2 or 3 inches to a giant of about 3 feet in length, enclosing perhaps a whole roast, a boned chicken or fish, or a pork loin.

What follows are several recipes for basic tamale dough. They are easy to make, and if you don't have corn husks handy, aluminum foil will do, or parchment paper (cut into 9×5-inch rectangles).

If you are using corn husks, place them in a bowl or pan and cover with hot water. Allow them to soak for at least 30 minutes (an hour or more is even better). Before using, rinse each husk and remove any corn silk. They should now be pliable enough to fold easily.

To Prepare Tamale Packages for Steaming

1. Dry corn husks and flatten them out in a single layer on a work surface or make a neat pile of smoothed and flattened husks.

2. Assemble one at a time. Place a spoonful of dough in the center of one husk and spread it out to an area about 3½ × 3 inches. Leave at least a 1-inch margin at the sides of the husk, 2 or more inches at top and bottom. The dough should be less than ¼ inch thick.

3. Place a little of whatever filling you're using over the middle of the dough and spread it out slightly with the back of a spoon, or with your fingers. Although not necessary, you can cover the filling with a little more dough if you like.

4. Fold in the sides of the husk toward the center, enclosing the filling completely. Then fold the pointed end of the husk over, and the broader end over that. With strips torn from an extra husk or with string, tie the tamale to keep the flaps securely closed. Do not tie too tightly (the dough expands while cooking).

NOTE: If you are using parchment, the procedure is the same. With foil, bring side edges together over the top of the filling and fold them twice, making a tight seal. Now fold the top and bottom up as above. Foil will keep its shape, so there is no need to tie the packages.

To Steam Tamales

1. Fill the bottom of a steamer with water up to the level indicated, (about 1 or 2 inches, depending on the size) and bring the water to a rolling boil.

2. Stand the tamales upright in the top of the steamer with the top flaps pointing down. Cover tamales with extra corn husks or a folded dish towel, and then with a tight-fitting lid. Slip the top of the steamer into the bottom.

3. Cook for 1 to 1½ hours, adding more water if it boils away. The tamales are done when they pull away easily from the husks, parchment, or foil. Test by removing one with tongs (be careful of the steam!) and open the package. The dough should be spongy and compact and not cling to the husk.

NOTE: Tamales can be served immediately or allowed to cool and reheated later. To reheat, simply place them in their husks on an ungreased griddle or heavy iron skillet over medium heat. Turn them until they are heated through. Foil-wrapped or parchment-wrapped tamales may be reheated in the oven for 20 minutes at 350°F.

Tamales freeze well. To heat, wrap still frozen husk-covered tamales in foil and place in a 350°F oven for 30 minutes. Foil or parchment-wrapped tamales should be spread on a cookie sheet and heated through in the same way.

Basic Tamale Doughs

TAMALE DOUGH I

2 cups Quaker *masa harina*
1 teaspoon baking powder
1 teaspoon salt
1½ cups lukewarm beef or chicken stock (homemade or canned), or water
½ cup solid shortening or lard

1. Mix the *masa harina*, baking powder, and salt in a bowl. Work in the stock with your hands until a soft, moist dough is formed.

2. In the bowl of an electric mixer, or by hand, beat the shortening or lard until fluffy (about 3 or 4 minutes). Add the dough, a little at a time, and beat until the mixture is spongy (about 3 minutes after the last addition, or until a small piece of dough placed on the surface of a cup of cold water floats. If it sinks, continue to beat until a piece of test dough floats).

3. Once the dough is prepared, follow the directions on page 30 for filling and steaming.

Makes about 2 dozen tamales

TAMALE DOUGH II

1 pound Quaker quick grits, ground to a fine powder in a food processor, blender, spice grinder, or electric coffee mill
1 teaspoon baking powder
1 teaspoon salt
½ cup solid shortening or lard
1½ cups lukewarm beef or chicken stock (homemade or canned), or water

1. Mix the ground grits, baking powder, and salt in a bowl.

2. With an electric mixer, or by hand, beat the shortening or lard until fluffy (about 3 or 4 minutes).

3. Alternately add the grits mixture and the stock to the shortening, beating all the while, until all ingredients are combined. Beat 2 or 3 minutes longer. Test a tiny piece of dough by floating it on the surface of a cup of cold water. If it sinks, keep beating until enough air is incorporated into the dough to make it float.

4. Once the dough is prepared, follow the directions above for filling and steaming.

Makes about 2 dozen tamales

TAMALE DOUGH III

2 cans (1 pound 13 ounces each) white hominy
1 small can (7 ounces) Green Giant Corn Niblets, drained well
1 teaspoon salt
1 teaspoon baking powder
½ cup solid shortening or lard

1. In two batches, grind the hominy and the corn niblets along with salt and baking powder in the workbowl of a food processor fitted with the steel blade.

2. With an electric mixer, or by hand, beat the shortening or lard until fluffy. Add the hominy mixture to the shortening and beat until well combined.

3. Once the dough is prepared, follow the directions above for filling and steaming.

Makes about 2 dozen tamales

Tamale dough is usually left unseasoned—the fillings add the flavor. But if you should serve unfilled, plain tamales (*tamales blancos*) as an accompaniment to a somewhat bland dish rather than as a separate course, you might want to add powdered or ground chilies to the dough, or a teaspoon of finely chopped fresh chili. Plain, unfilled tamales are wonderful when served with a spicy *mole* or a *picante* chicken or meat and chili dish. When making plain unfilled tamales, do not season the dough, just spread it *slightly* thicker on the husk, foil, or parchment.

Sweet or Breakfast Tamales: These are delicious with morning coffee or as a late-night snack. Use one of the Basic Tamale Dough recipes, substituting warm milk for the broth or stock, cutting the amount of salt in half, and replacing half the shortening with butter.

Fill sweet tamales with your favorite jam, preserves, chocolate bits, sweetened cottage cheese, raisins, or combinations of these, or with mixed cinnamon, sugar, nuts, and raisins; brown sugar, nuts, cinnamon, and apples sautéed in a little butter; peanut butter and jelly; almond paste and fresh banana bits; mango purée mixed with julienned orange rind; guava jelly softened with a little orange juice and mixed with shredded coconut; a tiny finger of fresh pineapple spread with a little cream cheese; and on and on, according to your whim or the sweet things you have at hand.

Sweet tamales can be made ahead, refrigerated, and reheated at the last minute.

Tamale Pie or Casserole: All you need to make a tamale pie is a 2-quart casserole, a Basic Tamale Dough recipe, and a savory filling like Picadillo (page 76), Mole Poblano (page 105), chicken, chilies, and so on.

If you wish, a richer dough can be made for a pie or casserole dish. Simply substitute ½ cup of light cream or half-and-half for part of the broth or stock; and butter, margarine, or rendered chicken fat for half the shortening called for.

After the dough is prepared:

1. Grease the casserole and line the sides and bottom with about two-thirds of the dough.

2. Fill with a recipe of your choice, and cover the top with the remaining dough, enclosing the filling completely. Place the pie in a preheated 350°F oven and bake for 1 hour. If you have more filling, save it for a future meal or serve, well heated, with portions of the pie.

SAUCES, DRESSINGS, AND FILLINGS

So, you know how to make tortillas and tamales. But what do you fill them with? What sauces do you spoon over your enchiladas? Which sauces do you serve on the side? Because sauces are indispensable to Mexican meals, sauces and relishes are as common to the Mexican table as ketchup and mustard bottles are to ours. The ketchup and mustard analogy is only half applicable, though, because you usually find ketchup and mustard on luncheonette counters and in fast food joints, and not in homes where food is well prepared and revered.

As we've discussed, Mexican food is not all *picante*, or hot. A lot of the heat—or a little of it—is often added at the table, according to taste.

Table sauces are what we're concerned with in this section. They are sometimes added to soups, or used with plain grilled meat or fish. A dollop can lend pungency to dry soups (*sopas secas*). A spoonful dribbled on a taco adds another bit of excitement.

There are fresh sauces and cooked sauces, bottled sauces and canned. They range from mild to searing. The ingredients are pretty much the same—combinations of tomatoes, chilies, avocados, herbs, spices, and other seasonings such as onions, garlic, and vinegar.

No Mexican table is complete without one or more bowls of the following sauces: Salsa Cruda (page 35), Salsa Verde (below), Salsa de Jitomate (page 34), Salsa de Chile Chipotle (page 35), Salsa de Chile Güero (below), Salsa Ranchera (page 35), Salsa de Chile Rojo (page 36).

SALSA VERDE
GREEN SAUCE

---

1 can (10 ounces) Mexican green tomatoes, drained
1 medium onion, finely chopped
2 canned *chiles serranos*, drained and chopped
2 cloves garlic, finely chopped
3 tablespoons fresh coriander, chopped
Salt and freshly ground pepper to taste

1. Place the green tomatoes in the workbowl of a food processor fitted with the steel blade. Pulse two or three times. Add the rest of the ingredients and pulse once or twice just to mix.
2. Pour into a serving bowl and taste for seasoning.

NOTE: If you like the taste, add more coriander leaves than the recipe calls for, or add more garlic and onions. Or omit garlic and onions completely. Change proportions according to your likes and dislikes—Mexicans do. Process salsa longer for a smooth, puréed texture.

Makes about 1½ cups

SALSA DE CHILE GÜERO
GREEN CHILI SAUCE

Use this sauce on any delicately flavored dish of fish, chicken, or eggs. The Güero chili, if used, makes a mild, almost gossamer sauce.

4 or 5 *chiles Güeros* (or California, Anaheim, or Poblano)
½ can (10 ounces) Mexican green tomatoes, drained
3 tablespoons fresh coriander, chopped
1 medium onion, finely chopped
2 cloves garlic, mashed
1 canned *chile serrano*, drained and chopped
¼ teaspoon sugar
Salt and freshly ground pepper to taste
3 tablespoons peanut, corn, or safflower oil

1. Plunge the chilies into boiling water and simmer for about 5 minutes. Drain; cut open and remove stems and seeds. Cut up roughly.

2. Place the chilies in the workbowl of a food processor fitted with the steel blade. Add all the other ingredients except the oil and pulse 3 or 4 times. Stop the machine and scrape down the sides with a spatula. Process for 2 or 3 seconds.

3. Heat the oil in a skillet; pour in the processed mixture. Cook over high heat, stirring constantly, for 2 or 3 minutes. Serve hot or cold.

Makes about 1½ cups

SALSA DE JITOMATE
RED TOMATO SAUCE

2 tablespoons peanut, corn, or safflower oil
1 medium to large onion, chopped
2 cloves garlic, thinly sliced
2 large fresh, ripe tomatoes, peeled, seeded, and chopped, or 4 canned
    whole tomatoes, drained and chopped
½ teaspoon sugar
3 canned *chiles serranos*, drained and chopped
Salt and freshly ground pepper to taste
1 tablespoon chopped coriander leaves

1. Heat the oil over high heat and sauté the onion and garlic, stirring, until the onion is translucent. Add the rest of the ingredients (except for the coriander). Cook over a low flame for 15 minutes, stirring occasionally. Add more salt and pepper if necessary.

2. Remove from the heat and add the chopped coriander; mix thoroughly. Serve either hot or cold.

Makes about 2 cups

SALSA DE CHILE CHIPOTLE

2 cups canned Italian plum tomatoes, partly drained
2 canned *chiles chipotles* with a little of the sauce
1½ tablespoons peanut, corn, or safflower oil
1 large onion, coarsely chopped

    1. Combine the tomatoes and chilies in the workbowl of a food processor fitted with the steel blade and process to a smooth purée.
    2. Heat the oil in a skillet and sauté the onion until translucent. Add the tomato-chili mixture and simmer, uncovered, stirring often, for about 15 minutes. Serve at room temperature.

Makes about 2½ cups

SALSA CRUDA
FRESH TOMATO SAUCE

You'll find this sauce as a condiment at almost every Mexican meal. It is used on cooked meats, fish, chicken, seafood, eggs, tacos, tostadas, enchiladas, and so on.

3 fresh, ripe tomatoes, peeled and chopped, or 6 canned Italian plum
    tomatoes, drained and chopped
3 canned *chiles serranos* or 2 *jalapeños,* drained and chopped
1 clove garlic, finely chopped
1 medium onion, finely chopped
1 tablespoon (or more) chopped coriander leaves
¼ teaspoon sugar
Salt and freshly ground pepper to taste

    1. Combine all the ingredients.
    2. Serve at room temperature, or store in the refrigerator in a tightly closed jar or plastic container and serve cold.

Makes about 2½ cups

SALSA RANCHERA
COUNTRY-STYLE SAUCE

A traditional sauce for Huevos Rancheros (page 116) and other egg dishes. This is very good spooned over a cheese soufflé.

2 tablespoons peanut, corn, or safflower oil
1 small onion, chopped
1 clove garlic, chopped
2 large fresh, ripe tomatoes, chopped, or 4 canned tomatoes, drained and
    chopped

1 can (12 ounces) *chiles jalapeños*, drained and finely chopped
1 teaspoon mild white vinegar
¼ teaspoon sugar
Salt and freshly ground pepper to taste

1. Heat the oil in a skillet and sauté the onion and garlic until translucent.

2. In the workbowl of a food processor fitted with the steel blade, process the tomatoes, chilies, vinegar, and sugar until puréed. Add to the onions and garlic in the skillet and cook down, uncovered, stirring occasionally, until thick and smooth. Add salt and pepper to taste. Serve warm or at room temperature.

Makes about 1½ cups

SALSA DE CHILE ROJO
RED CHILI SAUCE

This is a mild, classic sauce.

4 *chiles anchos*, prepared as directed on page 16
2 large fresh, ripe tomatoes, peeled, seeded, and chopped or 4 canned
    tomatoes, drained and chopped
1 large onion, chopped
2 cloves garlic, chopped
½ teaspoon dried oregano
3 tablespoons peanut, corn, or safflower oil
1 tablespoon mild white vinegar
Salt and freshly ground pepper to taste

1. Place all the ingredients except the oil, vinegar, salt, and pepper in the workbowl of a processor fitted with the steel blade. Pulse twice, then process for 2 or 3 seconds, or until smoothly puréed.

2. Heat the oil in a skillet; add the purée and cook, uncovered, for 5 minutes, stirring so the mixture doesn't stick.

3. Remove the purée from the heat; stir in the vinegar and season to taste with salt and pepper.

NOTE: Canned *chiles chipotles* or fresh *chiles jalapeños*—toasted over an open flame, peeled, and seeded—can be substituted for the *chiles anchos*. Follow the same cooking method. The result—*Salsa Chipotle*, or *Chipotle Chili Sauce*—is a much more fiery sauce.

Makes 2 cups

SALSA DE ALMENDRA VERDE
GREEN ALMOND SAUCE

Use this or the following almond sauce over string beans, peas, pasta, or grilled or broiled fish or chicken.

2 tablespoons light Italian olive oil or corn oil
1 cup coarsely chopped blanched almonds
3 tablespoons fresh bread crumbs
1 can (10 ounces) Mexican green tomatoes, drained
2 cloves garlic, chopped
2 tablespoons (or more) chopped coriander leaves
1 cup chicken stock (homemade or canned)
3 canned *chiles serranos,* drained and rinsed
Salt and freshly ground pepper to taste
¼ cup grated Parmesan or Romano cheese (optional)

1. Heat the oil in a skillet. Gently sauté the almonds and bread crumbs until golden brown.
2. Transfer the almonds and bread crumbs with a slotted spoon to the workbowl of a food processor fitted with the steel blade. Add the tomatoes, garlic, coriander, and chilies and process to a smooth purée.
3. Pour the mixture back into the skillet; add the stock and salt and pepper to taste and simmer, uncovered, stirring occasionally, for 5 minutes.
4. Remove the sauce from the heat; add the cheese and mix thoroughly. Refrigerated, this sauce will keep for up to 2 weeks.

Makes 2¼ cups

SALSA DE ALMENDRA ROJA
RED ALMOND SAUCE

2 tablespoons light Italian olive oil or corn oil
1 medium onion, finely chopped
2 cloves garlic, chopped
3 tablespoons fresh bread crumbs
½ cup coarsely chopped blanched almonds
½ teaspoon red pepper flakes
½ teaspoon dried oregano

1 fresh, ripe tomato, peeled and chopped, or 2 canned Italian plum
  tomatoes, drained and chopped
1½ cups chicken or beef stock (homemade or canned)
1 teaspoon lemon juice
½ teaspoon Maggi seasoning
Salt and freshly ground pepper to taste
¼ cup grated Parmesan or Romano cheese (optional)

1. Heat the oil in a skillet. Sauté the onion and garlic until translucent.
Add the bread crumbs, almonds, and pepper flakes and sauté, stirring, until they are golden brown.
2. Transfer this mixture to the workbowl of a food processor fitted with
the steel blade. Add the oregano, tomato, and stock and process to a smooth
purée.
3. Season the purée with lemon juice, salt, pepper, and Maggi and return
to the skillet. Simmer, uncovered, stirring occasionally, for 10 minutes.
4. Remove the sauce from the heat and add the cheese. Mix thoroughly.
Keeps well in the refrigerator for up to 2 weeks.

NOTE: You may substitute other nuts for the almonds—walnuts, pecans,
       cashews. Watch them as they cook, however, because some nuts
       brown faster than others.

Makes over 2 cups

GUACAMOLE

Guacamole is often used as a sauce, a salad, a first course served in hollowed-out tomatoes or, in this country especially, as a dip for *totopos* or
tostaditas (tortilla chips or triangles), and as a topping for tacos.

1 large, very ripe avocado
1 large fresh, ripe tomato, peeled, seeded, and chopped
1 clove garlic, minced
1 small onion, minced
2 canned *chiles serranos*, drained, seeded, and chopped
1 handful (less if you prefer) of chopped coriander leaves
Salt and freshly ground pepper to taste
¼ teaspoon sugar

1. Peel the avocado; remove and reserve the pit. Cut the flesh into large
pieces.
2. Place the avocado chunks, along with the rest of the ingredients, into
the workbowl of a food processor fitted with the steel blade. Pulse twice.
Remove the feed-tube cover and scrape down the sides with a spatula. The
mixture should be coarse, but with some of the avocado puréed. If too coarse,
pulse once more. Scrape into a serving dish and bury the pit in the center
(this is supposed to keep guacamole from turning dark). A more reliable
way, if you are not using the guacamole right away, is to cover it tightly—
with plastic wrap pressed against the mixture to keep air out—and refrigerate.

VARIATIONS: You may:

Add ½ red bell pepper, finely chopped, for color and crunch.

Substitute 2 or 3 scallions, chopped (green part included) for the onion. Fold in by hand.

Substitute ½ can Mexican green tomatoes, drained, for the red tomatoes.

Substitute canned *chiles chipotles en escabeche* for the *serranos*. Drain well and chop.

Serve in individual cocktail glasses with cold boiled shrimp arranged around the rim. Or cut ½ pound of cold boiled shrimp into chunks and add to the guacamole.

Makes about 2 cups

ANTOJITOS: APPETIZERS AND SNACKS

In Mexico, appetizers as we serve them in the U.S. are called *antojitos* ("little whims"). They are usually snacks that can be (and are) eaten throughout the day. Some tortilla dishes used as main dishes in the United States are merely snack food in Mexico: If it doesn't have a sauce poured over it, it's a snack.

Many recipes can be adapted easily for use as first courses or, when made with "cocktail-size" tortillas, can be passed with drinks before dinner. Make it in miniature and it goes with cocktails; make it full-sized and it's a first course or a main course. Some of these would include: Quesadillas (page 42), Tacos (page 42), Panuchos de Picadillo (page 43), Albóndigas (page 52), Albóndigas de Pescado (page 51), Frijoles Refritos (page 120), served with *totopos* or *tostaditas*, and so on. Fill hollowed cherry tomatoes with one of the Seviches (pages 45–47) or Guacamole (page 38) and serve as cocktail nibbles. Or turn *empañadas* into *empañaditas* stuffed with a variety of savory fillings. Form open-faced canapés called *sopes* or (cups of fried tortilla dough) in the shape of little boats (*chalupas*). These can be filled with chopped fried chorizos; with sauce and ground or shredded chicken, meat, or fish; with meats, chicken, or fish cooked in a sauce; with cheese and sauce; with sauce, meat, and sour cream topping; with cheese and chopped chilies melted under a broiler. These are merely a few suggestions; the list is almost endless and is limited only by your repertoire of Mexican foods and your imagination.

GORDAS ROJAS

Gordas are fat little dumplings, often stuffed with meat sauces or other fillings and eaten as snacks.

1½ cups Quaker *masa harina*
¾ cup water
½ teaspoon salt
1 *chile ancho*, prepared as directed on page 16, then ground to a powder in blender or food processor
Peanut, corn, or safflower oil for frying
Filling of your choice
Garnish of your choice

1. In a bowl mix the *masa harina* with the water, salt, and powdered *chile ancho*.
2. Divide the dough into 12 equal parts and roll each to form a ball. Flatten into round cakes about 2 inches across and ¼ inch thick.
3. Lightly oil a heavy skillet or sauté pan and set over medium heat. Sear

each of the cakes on one side; remove to a plate or work surface, seared side up, and pinch edges up to form little bowls or cups. Keep warm.

4. Pour oil into the skillet to $\frac{1}{4}$ inch and heat to the smoking point. Return the sopes to the hot oil, a few at a time, and fry, spooning oil into the cup to fry the interior as well. Remove the sopes as they become golden and drain on paper towels. Quickly fill them with any of the following:

Salsa de Jitomate (page 34), some chopped onion, grated Monterey Jack, and a dollop of sour cream.

Salsa Verde (page 33), slivers of cooked chicken, a sprinkling of ground almonds or pecans, and a dollop of sour cream or crème fraîche.

Crumbled and fried chorizos and grated Parmesan or a mild cheddar.

Sour cream, or crème fraîche, chopped pumpkin seeds, and chopped coriander.

Grated cheese (Monterey Jack, cheddar, or Havarti), and chopped fresh green chilies. Run under the broiler to melt the cheese and serve immediately topped with a spoonful of Salsa de Jitomate (page 34).

Leftover Picadillo (page 76), slivers of toasted almonds, and chopped green olives.

Frijoles Refritos (page 120), chopped chiles serranos, Salsa de Chile Güero (page 33), and grated Monterey Jack.

Serve surrounded with shredded lettuce, plus one or two of these: sliced radishes, diced jicama, chopped tomatoes, chopped onion, chopped egg.

Serves 6

GORDAS RELLENAS

Make dough for Gordas Rojas (above). After forming the dozen balls:

1. Press a $\frac{1}{2}$-inch square of Monterey Jack cheese into the center of each ball. Flatten a little and fry; drain on paper towels and serve.
2. Press a well into the center of each ball and fill with a teaspoon of Frijoles Refritos (page 120); flatten, fry, and drain as above.
3. Press some shredded chicken, moistened with a little picante sauce, into the center of the ball; flatten, fry, and drain as above.

Or, make dough for Gordas Rojas, substituting $\frac{3}{4}$ cup grated Parmesan for the chili (or in addition to the chili). Press a small piece of Carnitas (page 54) into the center of each ball; flatten, fry, and drain as above.

NOTE: These do not reheat well in the oven. Keep them warm for a few minutes before serving, if you must, in a 375°F oven (a low oven makes them soggy). Keep them too long and they will dry out. If you want to make them ahead, refry them very quickly, when serving, in very hot oil.

TACOS

These tacos are rolled and fried, Mexican-style, so they can be eaten easily without a fork.

Use 12 small (4 inch) tortillas. Stuff the tortillas with the mixture of your choice (see below) as directed on page 28.

Tacos de Picadillo. Make Picadillo (page 76), cutting the meat to 1 pound. Stuff the tacos and serve with Guacamole (page 38), shredded lettuce, and strips of canned green chilies (also called *rajas*).

Tacos de Chorizo. Remove the casings from 3 chorizos and fry the meat, crumbling it with a fork or spoon. In a bowl, combine chorizos with ½ cup shredded Monterey Jack or cheddar cheese. Stuff the tacos and serve with Guacamole (page 38), chopped tomatoes, and canned *chiles en escabeche.*

Tacos de Jamón. Combine in a bowl ½ pound chopped boiled ham; 1 small clove garlic, minced; 1 small onion, finely chopped; ¼ pound mild cheddar, mashed and softened; 2 crushed ripe, peeled tomatoes; and 1 canned *chile jalapeño*, chopped. Stuff the tacos and serve with Guacamole (page 38) and chopped coriander.

Use leftover Pollo Verde (page 91) or Mole Poblano (page 105). Stuff the tacos and serve with Guacamole (page 38) and sour cream or *crème fraîche.*

Tacos de Frijol. Stuff the tacos with Frijoles Refritos (page 120), strips of canned *chiles jalapeños* or *serranos*, and Havarti, Fontina, or Swiss cheese. Serve with Guacamole (page 38) and sour cream or *crème fraîche.*

Tacos de Pollo. Shred poached chicken breast; combine with some Salsa Verde (page 33), sour cream, or *crème fraîche*, chopped lettuce, and chopped scallion.

Makes 12 tacos

QUESADILLAS

Quesadillas are turnovers made from tortillas folded over to enclose a filling. These are usually toasted on a griddle or fried, but they can also be poached in broth and served with a sauce or added to soup. To make quesadillas from scratch:

Corn tortillas
Filling of your choice
½ cup corn oil

1. Make corn tortillas through step 3 as directed on page 26, but use a small ball of dough and peel off only one plastic sheet. Tortillas should be 3 or 4 inches in diameter.
2. Place a little filling of your choice (page 43) on one half of each tortilla not too near the edge.
3. Using the plastic wrap, fold tortillas over to form half-moons, with edges meeting.

4. Press the edges of the dough envelope together to seal.

5. Remove plastic and toast quesadilla on a hot griddle 3 or 4 minutes on each side, or fry to a golden brown in about ½ inch of oil (2 or 3 minutes on each side). Drain on paper toweling; serve immediately.

NOTE: When using store-bought small tortillas, omit plastic and prepare from step 3.

SUGGESTION: Use some of the same fillings suggested for Tacos (page 42) omitting the garnishes and steering clear of any stuffing that's too "wet." You may also try using:

Sautéed chopped mushrooms, onion, and chopped ham.

Fried and crumbled chorizo sausages mixed with a little mashed potato or Frijoles Refritos (page 120).

Ground pork, sautéed with lots of garlic, then combined with chopped string beans and diced potato.

Cubed mozzarella cheese, chopped green chilies, and some oregano.

Sautéed chopped onion and squash blossoms (trimmed of stems and green).

Any *picante* meat dish such as Picadillo (page 76), and Carnitas (page 54), or shredded meat or chicken with a spoonful of thick sauce.

PANUCHOS
MEXICAN PITA

Panuchos are a filling appetizer and could be served as a light luncheon or supper dish. *Panuchos* are often topped with a little shredded meat or chicken and garnished with fresh or pickled onion rings.

12 small (3 or 4 inches) corn tortillas
Filling of your choice
½ cup corn oil

1. Puff tortillas up on a hot griddle.
2. Open each tortilla to form a pocket by inserting the tip of a sharp knife into one of the blisters on the tortilla and making a slit about a quarter of the way around, taking care not to pierce either the top or bottom "skin."
3. Stuff with filling of your choice and deep fry in ½ inch of hot oil.

FILLING:
1 cup Frijoles Refritos (page 120), preferably made with black beans
3 hard boiled eggs, sliced
1 boneless chicken breast, poached, shredded
Pickled Onion (page 44)
Peanut, corn, or safflower oil for frying

1. Spread the inside of each pocket with about 1 teaspoon of refried beans.
2. Place a slice of egg on top of beans; press to close the pocket.
3. Fry a few at a time in ¼ inch of hot oil in a heavy skillet or sauté pan, bottom side down. Turn and fry briefly on other side, or spoon hot oil over top of *panucho* to cook. Drain. To serve, sprinkle with shredded chicken and top with some pickled onion rings.

Serves 6

CEBOLLA EN ESCABECHE
PICKLED ONION

This condiment must marinate overnight.

½ cup water
1 large purple onion, thinly sliced
Salt
3 fresh *chiles serranos* or *jalapeños*, halved
½ teaspoon dried oregano
½ teaspoon ground cumin
1 bay leaf
2 cloves garlic, quartered
½ teaspoon peppercorns
½ cup mild white vinegar

1. In a saucepan, immerse the sliced onions in salted water for 5 minutes.
2. Add the remaining ingredients and bring to a rolling boil; remove from the heat and allow to cool.
3. Store the mixture in a glass jar in the refrigerator overnight. Keeps for weeks.

NOTE: Pickled onion is not only used for garnishing *panuchos*, but for salads, other *antojitos*, meats, and tacos as well. (We often pickle a whole head of garlic with the onions. Thus cooked, pickled onion is used as garnish and is a delicious addition to Mexican *bolillos* or French hard rolls and butter.)

Makes 1 cup

BOLILLITOS DE PAN RELLENOS
STUFFED ROLLS

These are little stuffed rolls. Mexican rolls (*bolillos*) are the best we've ever tasted—anywhere—and they cost only about a penny apiece! Their crunchy crusts are incomparable and the interiors are light and flaky. You can substitute hard French rolls.

6 hard French rolls
4 tablespoons butter
1 clove garlic, finely minced
3 romaine lettuce leaves, shredded
2 tablespoons vinaigrette dressing
2 chorizo sausages, fried and crumbled
1 Idaho potato, diced, cooked
1 medium onion, finely chopped
2 eggs beaten, fried, and thinly shredded
Salt and freshly ground pepper to taste
1 cup Frijoles Refritos (page 120)
1 cup Salsa Verde (page 33)
Grated Parmesan cheese
2 radishes, thinly sliced

1. Cut one-third off the tops of the French rolls (save them) and pull out the inside of the bottom section of the roll.

2. Invert roll and fry both parts in a portion of butter seasoned with the garlic. Remove from the heat.

3. Place a layer of shredded lettuce, tossed with a little vinaigrette dressing, in the bottom of each roll.

4. Then place a layer of fried, crumbled chorizo sausages, along with some cooked diced potatoes and finely chopped onion, in the roll.

5. Add the thinly shredded and fried egg, salt and pepper to taste, some *frijoles refritos*, a little *salsa verde*, a sprinkling of grated Parmesan, and a couple of thin slices of radish.

6. Put the top back on and enjoy while hot.

Variations, equally delicious, are the fillings recommended for Tacos (page 42), Quesadillas (page 42), and Panuchos (page 43). Or try crab meat sautéed with chopped onion, salt and pepper, combined with some heavy cream, minced *chile jalapeño*, a pinch of dry mustard, and a dash of Maggi seasoning. Pack the mixture into fried hard rolls, top with grated Parmesan or cheddar cheese, and run under the broiler before putting on its lid and serving.

NOTE: To serve with drinks, cut a small roll in half lengthwise, hollow out each side, fry, and stuff. Serve without a lid.

Serves 6

SEVICHE

Although *seviche* originated in Peru (by way of the Polynesian Islands), it has metamorphosed into a dish so Mexican that it is considered one of the country's national foods. There are many versions and many spellings of the name. It is a wonderful first course, or can make colorful bite-sized canapés when stuffed into hollowed-out cherry tomatoes.

Seviche I

The fish in this recipe must marinate 5 or 6 hours.

1 pound firm, white-fleshed fish, filleted and cut into cubes about ½ to ¾
   inch
Juice of 6 limes (about ½ cup)
2 tomatoes, peeled, seeded, and diced (fresh only and red ripe)
1 medium onion, finely chopped
2 *chiles jalapeños* (fresh or canned), seeded and cut into small dice
¼ cup light Italian olive oil
1 tablespoon mild white vinegar
¼ cup chopped coriander leaves
1 teaspoon freshly ground pepper
Salt to taste
½ teaspoon dried oregano
2 tablespoons capers

   1. Place the cubed fish in a deep glass or stainless-steel bowl and cover
with lime juice. Marinate in the refrigerator for about 5 or 6 hours to "cook."
Toss once or twice during the "cooking" process. The fish will turn white,
opaque, and become even firmer textured.
   2. Remove the fish from the refrigerator and drain, reserving the lime juice.
   3. Combine the rest of the ingredients with the reserved juice; pour over
the fish and toss. Refrigerate until serving time.

Serves 6 as an appetizer,
or 4 as a luncheon main dish

Seviche II

The scallops in this recipe must marinate at least 2 hours.

1 pound bay scallops (or sea scallops cut into small pieces)
Juice of 6 limes (about ½ cup)
2 fresh, ripe tomatoes, peeled, seeded, and diced
1 medium onion, finely chopped
1 clove garlic, minced
1 small bell pepper (green or red), seeded, diced small
1 ripe avocado, peeled and cubed
2 *chiles serranos* or *jalapeños* (fresh or canned), seeded and finely
   chopped
¼ cup chopped coriander leaves
¼ cup light Italian olive oil
Salt to taste
½ teaspoon freshly ground pepper

1. Marinate the scallops in lime juice for 2 hours or more in the refrigerator.

2. Combine the other ingredients and add them to the scallops and juice. Toss lightly. Return to the refrigerator until serving time. Serve cold.

Serves 6

Seviche III

The seafood in this recipe must marinate 4 or more hours.

½ pound bay scallops (or sea scallops cut into small pieces)
½ pound shrimp, shelled and deveined
½ pound mackerel, sole, striped bass, or halibut fillets
Juice of 12 limes (about 1 cup)
1 medium onion, minced
1 small bell pepper (green or red), seeded and minced
2 cloves garlic, minced
1 fresh *chile jalapeño*, seeded and minced
2 teaspoons coriander leaves, minced
2 sweet gherkins, minced
Salt and freshly ground pepper to taste
1 teaspoon sugar
½ cup mild white vinegar
1 large ripe avocado

1. Cut the seafood into tiny pieces.

2. Combine the seafood in a bowl with the lime juice. Cover and refrigerate for 4 hours or more until the seafood is an opaque white and looks "cooked."

3. Drain off and discard the lime juice; dry the seafood with paper toweling.

4. Combine the remaining ingredients (except the avocado) in a bowl. Taste for seasoning; the mixture should be sweet and spicy. Add the drained seafood and toss well. Return to the refrigerator until serving time.

5. Before serving, peel and dice the avocado, and combine with the seafood mixture.

Serves 6 to 8 as an appetizer,
or 4 as a luncheon or supper dish

ESCABECHE MAYA

Cooked Seviche from the Yucatán.

1 pound halibut, sole, or mackerel fillets
2 tablespoons lime juice

All-purpose flour
Salt and freshly ground pepper to taste
2 tablespoons peanut, corn, or safflower oil
4 cloves garlic, crushed through a press
2 medium onions, sliced
3 canned tomatoes, drained and crushed, or 3 fresh, ripe tomatoes, peeled, seeded, and chopped
2 bay leaves
½ teaspoon ground allspice
½ teaspoon grated nutmeg
½ teaspoon ground cumin
Pinch of ground cinnamon
½ cup mild white vinegar
¼ teaspoon cayenne pepper
1 tablespoon light Italian olive oil
Sliced radishes, capers, and shredded lettuce for garnish (optional)

1. Cut the fillets into strips about 2×1 inches and place in a shallow baking dish in one layer. Pour the lime juice over and allow to marinate for 1 hour, turning the fillets 2 or 3 times.

2. Drain the lime juice from the fillets into a saucepan and set aside. Dry the fillets with paper toweling and dust lightly with flour seasoned with salt and pepper.

3. Heat the oil in a skillet or sauté pan and fry the fillet pieces until they are just cooked through, about 3 or 4 minutes. Remove with a slotted spoon and place in a serving dish.

4. Combine the rest of the ingredients, except for the optional garnishes, in the saucepan with the reserved lime juice and bring to a boil. Lower the heat and simmer until the onions are soft and transparent.

5. Pour the liquid over the fish and allow to cool. Refrigerate for 24 hours.

6. Remove the bay leaves and serve the *seviche* as a first course garnished with sliced radishes, a sprinkling of capers, and shredded lettuce if desired.

Serves 6

MANTEQUILLA DE CACAHUATES
PEANUT BUTTER

1 tablespoon (a little more if necessary) peanut oil
5 cloves garlic, minced
1½ cups roasted peanuts
1 teaspoon salt (or to taste)
1 teaspoon cayenne pepper
1 teaspoon coarsely ground pepper
½ teaspoon sugar

1. Heat 1 tablespoon oil in a heavy skillet large enough to keep the peanuts moving; add the garlic and peanuts. Sauté for 2 minutes, stirring constantly; add the salt, peppers, and sugar and combine well. Remove from the heat and allow to cool.

2. Place the cooled peanut mixture in the workbowl of a food processor fitted with the steel blade and process to a smooth paste. Add a little more oil if the paste is too thick. Serve with crackers.

Makes about 1¼ to 1½ cups

HONGOS ESCABECHADOS
PICKLED MUSHROOMS

This condiment must marinate 6 hours or overnight.

1 onion, thinly sliced
Salt, to taste
1 *chile jalapeño* (canned or fresh), seeded and sliced into thin rings
¼ teaspoon dried oregano
¼ teaspoon ground cumin
2 cloves garlic, thinly sliced
½ cup mild white vinegar
½ cup water
1 pound fresh mushrooms, quartered
½ pint dairy sour cream
Freshly ground pepper to taste
Lettuce leaves for garnish

1. Place all ingredients (except for mushrooms, sour cream, and pepper) in a saucepan. Bring to a rolling boil; remove from the heat and add the mushrooms.
2. Cool, then refrigerate for 6 hours or overnight.
3. Before serving, remove the ingredients from the marinade to a bowl with a slotted spoon and mix with the sour cream. Sprinkle with freshly ground pepper. Serve on lettuce leaves.

Serves 6 to 8 as an appetizer

PAPAS RELLENAS CON JAIBAS
NEW POTATOES STUFFED WITH CRAB MEAT

24 small new potatoes boiled in their skins
2 tablespoons butter
1 medium onion, finely chopped
1 clove garlic, minced
½ *chile jalapeño* (fresh or canned), chopped
½ pound crab meat, flaked
½ teaspoon dry mustard
1 tablespoon finely chopped coriander leaves
2 tablespoons dry sherry
Salt and freshly ground pepper to taste
½ cup (or as needed) heavy cream
Grated Parmesan cheese

1. Cut a tiny slice from one end of each potato so that it can stand. With a melon-ball scoop or demitasse spoon, scoop out a depression in the opposite end of each potato, leaving a cuplike shell. Mash scoopings and set aside.

2. In a skillet, melt the butter and sauté the onion, garlic, and *chile jalapeño* for a few minutes until the onion is translucent. Stir in the potato and crab meat; add the sherry and turn the heat to high. Cook until liquid is absorbed. Season with salt and pepper.

3. Remove from the heat and add the mustard and coriander leaves and just enough cream to hold the mixture together.

4. Heap a spoonful of the crab meat into each of the potatoes, sprinkle with Parmesan, and run under the broiler for 2 or 3 minutes. Serve immediately as a first course, or as a snack with drinks.

Serves 6

CAMARONES FRIOS Y AGUACATE EN MAYONESA
COLD SHRIMP AND AVOCADO IN PICANTE MAYONNAISE

1 pound medium shrimp
4 cups water
1 teaspoon salt
½ teaspoon dried thyme or *epazote*
½ bay leaf
1 teaspoon white mustard seeds
1 teaspoon mild white vinegar
1 large ripe avocado
Picante Mayonnaise (page 51)
Capers
Watercress, lettuce leaves, or hollowed-out fresh, ripe tomatoes (optional)

1. Peel and devein the shrimp; rinse well.
2. Place the shrimp in the water with the salt, thyme or *epazote*, bay leaf, mustard seeds, and vinegar in a large pot; bring to a boil over high heat.
3. Add the shrimp; turn the heat down to medium and simmer for 3 to 5 minutes, until pink. Drain and set in the refrigerator to chill.
4. Peel and cut the avocado into medium-sized cubes.
5. Place the shrimp in a bowl; mix in the mayonnaise to coat the shrimp completely. Fold in the avocado cubes gently so as not to squash. May be refrigerated for several hours before serving. Serve on individual plates, sprinkled with capers. If desired, nest in a bed of watercress, lettuce leaves, or in hollowed-out tomatoes.

Serves 6

PICANTE MAYONNAISE

1 cup mayonnaise
¼ cup Dijon mustard
1 teaspoon lime juice
2 scallions, with greens, finely chopped
2 tablespoons chopped coriander or parsley leaves
1 tablespoon *chile jalapeño* (fresh or canned), seeded and finely chopped
1 tablespoon finely chopped capers
½ teaspoon dried oregano

1. In a small bowl, whisk together the mayonnaise, mustard, and lime juice until well combined.
2. Fold in the rest of the ingredients.

NOTE: Use this sauce with any cooked and chilled shellfish, such as mussels, scallops, raw clams, or oysters. It is also good with fried seafood and as a dip for raw vegetables and Albóndigas de Pescado (see below).

Makes about 1½ cups

ALBÓNDIGAS DE PESCADO
FISH BALLS

3 pounds firm, white-fleshed fish fillets (sole, halibut, or mackerel cut in small pieces)
¼ cup mild white vinegar
2 slices fresh white bread
1 small onion, coarsely chopped
2 medium-sized fresh, ripe tomatoes, peeled, seeded, and cut coarsely, or 4 canned Italian plum tomatoes, drained
2 cloves garlic, cut in quarters
1 tablespoon chopped parsley
3 eggs, lightly beaten
2 fresh *chiles poblanos* (California, Anaheim, or Güero), toasted, peeled, seeded, deveined, and cut into small pieces
½ cup chopped pitted black olives (optional)
Salt and freshly ground pepper
2 eggs
¼ cup all-purpose flour
1 cup fresh bread crumbs
Peanut, corn, or safflower oil for deep frying

1. Place the fish in the workbowl of a food processor fitted with the steel blade and process until smooth.
2. Soak the bread in the vinegar, and add to the workbowl along with the onion, tomatoes, garlic, parsley, and eggs. Season with salt and pepper and pulse once or twice until thoroughly combined.
3. Form the mixture into balls about 1 to 1½ inches in diameter. Place on a plate, cover with plastic wrap, and refrigerate for one hour.

4. Beat the eggs in a bowl.

5. Have the flour and bread crumbs in separate piles on a sheet of waxed paper. Dredge each fish ball in flour, then dip into the eggs, covering all the surfaces. Last, roll the ball in bread crumbs. (Use two forks if you find this procedure too messy to do with your hands.)

6. Chill the fish balls again for several hours.

7. Heat the oil in a deep pot or deep-fat fryer; it should register 360°F on a deep-fry thermometer. With a slotted spoon, drop several balls at a time into the oil (without crowding them). Fry, turning once or twice, until golden brown, about 4 or 5 minutes. Remove to paper toweling to drain. Serve hot, skewered on toothpicks, with Picante Mayonnaise (page 51) on the side, or with Salsa Cruda (page 35) for dipping.

VARIATION: Albóndigas de Pescado may be poached in a tomato sauce and served as a first course or main dish. For the sauce:

> ¼ cup light Italian olive oil
> 1 medium onion, chopped
> 3 pounds fresh, ripe tomatoes, peeled, seeded, and chopped,
>   or 1 can (35 ounces) Italian plum tomatoes, drained
> Small handful of parsley
> ½ teaspoon dried thyme
> 1 canned *chile chipotle en escabeche,* drained and sliced
> Salt and freshly ground pepper to taste

1. Heat the olive oil in a heavy saucepan and sauté the onion until golden. Add the tomatoes, parsley, thyme, and chili and simmer, uncovered, stirring occasionally, for 5 to 10 minutes, until the sauce thickens slightly. Season with salt and pepper.

2. Omitting the coating and frying procedure, add the fish balls to the tomato sauce and poach for 15 to 20 minutes. Serve with Arroz Blanco (page 66) if desired.

Makes 36 fish balls

ALBÓNDIGAS
MEATBALLS

1 pound ground beef (top or bottom round)
1 pound ground lean pork
¼ cup fresh bread crumbs
¼ cup milk
1 egg, beaten
1 teaspoon dried oregano
1 teaspoon dried thyme
¼ cup minced parsley
1 teaspoon salt
1 teaspoon freshly ground pepper
Pitted green olives
¼ cup peanut, corn, or safflower oil

1. Combine the beef and pork.

2. Soak the bread crumbs in milk for a few minutes and mix into the meat. Add the egg, oregano, thyme, parsley, salt, and pepper. Mix well and form into balls (about 1½ inches in diameter). Press an olive into the center of each ball.

3. In a heavy skillet or sauté pan, heat the oil to smoking and sauté the meatballs until browned. Serve on toothpicks, with warm Salsa de Chile Güero (page 33) for dipping.

Makes 36 meatballs

ALBÓNDIGAS EN SALSA DE JITOMATES
MEATBALLS IN TOMATO SAUCE

Prepare 36 Albóndigas (meatballs) as described in previous recipe, through step 2. Set aside and make the sauce.

1 can (35 ounces) Italian plum tomatoes, with liquid
1 canned *chile chipotle en escabeche*, drained and chopped
2 tablespoons peanut, corn, or safflower oil
1 medium onion, chopped
2 cloves garlic, minced
2 cups beef broth (homemade or canned)
Salt and freshly ground pepper to taste

1. In a blender or food processor, purée the tomatoes with the chili.

2. Heat the oil in a large saucepan or sauté pan and sauté the onion and garlic until golden. Pour in the puréed tomatoes and cook over medium heat 3 or 4 minutes, stirring constantly. Pour in the broth and mix thoroughly.

4. Drop the meatballs into the sauce and simmer for 30 minutes. Serve with rice or noodles.

Serves 6 generously

ALMEJAS EN MAYONESA PICANTE
MUSSELS IN PICANTE MAYONNAISE

4 pounds mussels
1 large onion, coarsely chopped
2 celery stalks, with leaves, coarsely chopped
1 bay leaf, split in half
2 whole cloves
4 cloves garlic, minced
1½ cups dry white wine
2 sprigs parsley
Salt and freshly ground pepper to taste
Picante Mayonnaise (page 51)

1. Scrub the mussels, pull off beards, and rinse in several changes of water.

2. Place the onion, celery, bay leaf, cloves, garlic, white wine, parsley, salt, and pepper in a large deep sauté pan, stockpot, or fish poacher over high heat and bring to a boil. Add the mussels, cover and cook over medium heat for about 10 minutes, or until the shells open. Shake the pot frequently or stir the mussels with a wooden spoon during cooking. When done, allow to cool in the broth.

3. Remove the mussels with a slotted spoon. Remove one side of each shell and discard. Loosen mussel in other shell. Spread each mussel with about ½ teaspoon of mayonnaise. Arrange in concentric circles on a serving platter. Serve cold.

NOTE: Reserve broth and serve as soup at another meal (there will be about 4 cups; the mussels give off a lot of liquid).

Serves 6

CARNITAS
BITES OF BROWNED MEAT

3 pounds boneless pork shoulder with some fat
Cold water to cover
1 tablespoon salt
Freshly ground pepper to taste
½ teaspoon ground cumin
½ teaspoon dried oregano
2 cloves garlic, minced
¼ teaspoon cayenne pepper
Peanut, corn, or safflower oil (optional)

1. Cut the meat into strips about 2 inches long and ½ inch square. Do not cut away the fat.

2. Place the pork in a heavy sauté pan. Add water (just to cover), salt, and pepper and bring to a boil.

3. Lower heat a bit and continue to cook until all the liquid has evaporated. The meat should be tender and the fat should begin to render out. Add the cumin, oregano, garlic, and cayenne. Stir thoroughly.

4. Stir the meat and continue cooking until each piece is browned, turning pieces often. This should take another 15 to 30 minutes. If there is not enough fat to brown the meat properly, add a little oil. If you like, serve with tortillas and Guacamole (page 38), Salsa Cruda (page 35), Salsa Verde (page 33), or Salsa de Jitomate (page 34). Or just with toothpicks and cocktails.

Serves 6–12

CARNE COSIDA
MARINATED MEAT

This is Mexico's steak tartare, a *seviche*-like concoction made with beef instead of fish. It is a delicious accompaniment to a glass of cold Mexican beer.

Juice of 6 limes (about ½ cup)
1 pound ground sirloin, trimmed of *all* fat
1 medium onion, finely chopped
1 clove garlic, minced
1 medium fresh, ripe tomato, peeled, seeded, and chopped
3 *chiles serranos* (canned or fresh), seeded and finely chopped
1 tablespoon mild white vinegar
½ teaspoon dried oregano
Salt and freshly ground pepper to taste
1 tablespoon finely chopped coriander leaves

1. Combine the lime juice and ground sirloin in a bowl and set in the refrigerator to "cook" for 3 or 4 hours or overnight.
2. Mix the rest of the ingredients into the meat and allow to season for another hour or two in the refrigerator. If desired, serve with fried tortillas, either whole small ones, or triangles.

Serves 4–6

JÍCAMA STICKS

1 small jícama
1 lime
Salt

1. Peel the jícama. Cut in ½-inch slices, then cut each slice into ½-inch sticks.
2. Squeeze the lime juice over the sticks and sprinkle with salt. Toss and serve.

NOTE: Powdered chili may also be sprinkled—sparsely—over the sticks.

Serves 6–12

BOTANAS DE CAMARONES
SHRIMP FRITTERS

1 pound medium shrimp
1 cup all-purpose flour
1 cup cornstarch
3 teaspoons baking powder
½ cup peanut, corn, or safflower oil

1 to 1¼ cups cold water
1 medium onion, finely chopped
2 or 3 *chiles jalapeños* (fresh or canned), chopped
Peanut oil for deep frying

1. Peel and devein the shrimp; rinse and dry thoroughly with paper toweling. Cut into small pieces. Set aside.

2. Place the flour, cornstarch, and baking powder in a bowl and gradually whisk in the oil. The batter will be quite thick. Start whisking in the water until the mixture thins to the consistency of pancake batter. Fold in the shrimp pieces, the onion, and the chopped chilies.

3. In a deep-fryer or a deep pot, heat the peanut oil to 375°F on a deep-fry thermometer. Drop tablespoons of the mixture, one at a time, into the hot oil. Fry 3 or 4 at a time. Fry for 2 or 3 minutes, turning to brown all sides. Do not crowd the pot or risk reducing the temperature too much or the fritters will absorb oil. When golden, drain on paper toweling.

VARIATIONS: For snacks to serve with drinks, drop the batter into hot oil by the teaspoonful. Serve these miniature fritters with a mild chili sauce for dipping.

Substitute scallops, cut into bits, for the shrimp.

Serves 6 as a first course

SOPAS: SOUPS

Mexicans love soups, especially at the midday meal. It wasn't always this way, however. Evidence seems to prove that Indians in pre-Cortés Mexico did not list soups among their meal courses. The Spaniards must have introduced soups to Mexico; the Indians and subsequent invading cultures put their own distinctive stamps on them.

One of the most popular soups in Mexico is tortilla soup. Then there are the green soups (like lime or avocado), the yellow soups (squash blossom, bean, garlic), the multicolored soups (vegetable, tomato and corn, fish with herbs, tomatoes, and chick-peas). Complete-meal soups (with meat, vegetables, and potatoes) are fortified with sauces, raw diced vegetables and fruits for crunch, and the surprise of thyme, cinnamon, cloves, and allspice.

SOPA DE AGUACATE
AVOCADO SOUP

3 large (or 5 medium) ripe avocados
Salt and freshly ground pepper to taste
1 cup heavy cream
2 tortillas (corn or wheat)
2 tablespoons peanut, corn, or safflower oil
2 tablespoons butter
1 medium onion, finely chopped
6 cups chicken stock (homemade or canned)
½ cup dry sherry
1 tablespoon finely chopped coriander leaves

1. Peel the avocados, cut into chunks, and place in the workbowl of a food processor fitted with the steel blade. Purée.

2. Add salt and a generous amount of freshly ground pepper and the heavy cream to the workbowl. Pulse once or twice to combine thoroughly. Set aside.

3. Cut the tortillas into 1-inch squares and fry in the oil until golden. Drain on paper toweling.

4. In a large saucepan, melt the butter and sauté the onion until translucent. Add the chicken stock, sherry, and coriander and bring to a boil.

5. Pour the avocado mixture into a tureen. Correct the seasoning of the boiling stock and pour over the avocado purée; mix well. Ladle into individual soup bowls. Sprinkle with a few tortilla squares and pass additional tortilla squares.

VARIATION: This soup is also delicious cold. Cook the broth as above and chill. Before serving, purée the avocados with cream and combine with broth. Sprinkle with chopped scallions in place of the tortilla squares, or omit the cream when puréeing the avocados and serve the soup with a dollop of sour cream or *crème fraîche* and a sprinkling of minced coriander leaves.

Serves 6

SOPA DE ELOTE
CORN SOUP

1 medium onion, finely chopped
2 tablespoons butter
6 canned Italian plum tomatoes, drained
2½ cups cooked corn kernels (or canned Green Giant Corn Niblets, drained)
4 cups chicken stock (homemade or canned)
Salt and freshly ground pepper to taste
1 cup heavy cream

1. Sauté the onion in the butter until golden.
2. Transfer the onion to the workbowl of a food processor fitted with the steel blade, along with the tomatoes, 2 cups corn kernels (reserve ½ cup for garnish), and 1 cup of the stock. Purée.
3. In a saucepan, combine the purée with the remaining stock; season with salt and pepper to taste and bring to a boil. Reduce the heat and simmer for about 10 minutes.
4. Whisk the cream into the mixture. Taste and adjust the seasoning. Serve sprinkled with the reserved corn.

VARIATION: For Sopa de Elote con Pimientos (Corn Soup with Sweet Red Peppers), reduce the quantity of corn to 2 cups and add 3 canned pimientos to the processor and purée. Continue the recipe as above, omitting the corn garnish. Sprinkle each bowl of soup with a little paprika.

Serves 6

SOPA DE ALBÓNDIGAS
MEATBALL SOUP

Albóndigas (page 52), uncooked
2 tablespoons peanut, corn, or safflower oil
1 medium onion, finely chopped
6 cups beef stock (homemade or canned)
2 cloves garlic, minced
1 cup tomato purée (fresh or canned)
Salt and freshly ground pepper to taste

1. Make the *albóndigas*.
2. Heat the oil in a skillet and sauté the onion until golden.
3. Heat the beef stock in a large saucepan or soup pot and add the onion, along with the garlic and tomato purée. Season with salt and pepper and bring to a boil. Add the meatballs and turn the heat down to simmer. Cover the pot and cook until meatballs are cooked through, or about 45 minutes. Serve hot.

Serves 6

SOPA DE FLOR DE CALABAZA
SQUASH BLOSSOM SOUP

A delicate soup made from zucchini flowers.

1 pound squash blossoms
4 tablespoons butter
1 small onion, finely chopped
6 cups chicken stock (homemade or canned)
1 bay leaf
Salt and freshly ground pepper to taste

1. Remove the stems from the blossoms. Chop the blossoms roughly.
2. Heat the butter in a saucepan and sauté the onion until limp. Add the squash blossoms and sauté a few minutes more. Add the chicken stock and bay leaf and cook 10 minutes.
3. Before serving, pick out the bay leaf and discard. Ladle the soup into heated bowls.

NOTE: Authentic squash blossom soup is made with a sprig of *epazote*, added at the last minute. If you can find it, forget the bay leaf and use the *epazote*.

Serves 6

SOPA DE AJO
GARLIC SOUP

2 tablespoons peanut, corn, or safflower oil
1 large head garlic, each clove peeled and halved
6 cups chicken stock (homemade or canned)
Salt and freshly ground pepper to taste
3 eggs, well beaten with a few drops of oil
6 slices (1½ inches thick) fresh white bread
¼ cup peanut, corn, or safflower oil

1. Heat the oil in a skillet and sauté the garlic cloves for 30 seconds. Turn off the heat or remove skillet from stove.

59

2. In a saucepan, heat the chicken stock to the boiling point, then turn the heat down to medium.

3. Remove the garlic from the skillet with a slotted spoon and transfer to the workbowl of a food processor fitted with the steel blade. (Reserve the skillet with the oil.) Add some of the hot stock (about ½ cup) to the garlic and purée. Stir the purée into the simmering stock. Add salt and pepper, cover, and continue simmering for 20 minutes.

4. Remove the cover and stir the broth while pouring the egg into it. The egg should form ribbons and strands similar to egg drop soup. Cover and simmer until the eggs are set.

5. Fry the bread slices in the oil until both sides are golden brown and crisp. Drain briefly on paper toweling; place one in each of 6 soup bowls and ladle the hot soup over.

Serves 6

SOPA DE LEGUMBRES
VEGETABLE SOUP

6 small zucchini
1 large onion, chopped
6 carrots, scraped and sliced
6 small potatoes, pared and diced
1 can (16 ounces) Italian plum tomatoes, with liquid
6 cups chicken stock (homemade or canned)
1 bay leaf
Salt and freshly ground pepper to taste
1 large ripe avocado, peeled and cut in strips, for garnish

1. Cut the zucchini into ¼-inch slices.

2. Place the zucchini and the other vegetables in the stock with the bay leaf. Bring to a boil, then reduce the heat to simmering. Season the soup with salt and pepper; cover and simmer until the tomatoes disintegrate and the rest of the vegetables are tender, about 30 minutes.

3. Remove the bay leaf before serving. Ladle into individual soup bowls and garnish with strips of avocado.

Serves 6

SOPA DE POLLO Y PACANAS
CHICKEN AND PECAN SOUP

½ cup coarsely broken pecan meats
2 tablespoons butter
1 large onion, finely chopped
2 carrots, scraped and cut in tiny dice
1 cup shredded lettuce
2 whole chicken breasts, skinned and boned

8 cups chicken stock (homemade or canned)
Salt and freshly ground pepper to taste
¼ teaspoon ground allspice
¼ cup dry sherry
1 tablespoon chopped parsley
2 scallions, with greens, chopped

1. In a large saucepan or soup pot, sauté the pecans briefly in butter. Add the onion, carrots, lettuce, chicken breasts, and chicken stock; season with salt and pepper and simmer for 30 minutes, or until breasts are tender.

2. Remove the chicken breasts from the liquid and cut one into chunks. Cut the other into bite-sized pieces.

3. Place chunks (not pieces) and a ladleful of stock into the workbowl of a food processor fitted with the steel blade and purée.

4. Return puréed mixture to stock, along with the bite-sized pieces of chicken breast. Add the allspice and sherry and heat through but do not boil. Serve in soup bowls, sprinkled with parsley and scallions.

VARIATIONS: Sprinkle each bowl generously with grated Parmesan instead of scallions.

Add ½ cup of tiny pasta (ditalini, orzo, or pastina) to the stock along with the puréed chicken breast. Simmer for 10 minutes longer.

Substitute ½ cup blanched whole almonds, walnuts, or skinned and sautéed filberts for the pecans.

Serves 6

SOPA DE PAPA
POTATO SOUP

4 tablespoons sweet butter
1½ pounds onions, sliced
4 large baking potatoes, pared and cubed
6 cups chicken stock (fresh or canned)
½ cup chopped parsley
Salt and freshly ground pepper to taste
1 cup sour cream or *crème fraîche*
1 small can (4 ounces) chopped green chilies, drained

1. In a large saucepan or soup pot, heat the butter until it foams, and sauté onions until lightly browned. Mix in the cubed potatoes, then add the chicken stock, parsley, and generous amounts of salt and pepper. Cover the pot and simmer for 30 minutes.

2. In a bowl, combine the sour cream and green chilies. Mix in a ladleful of the soup, then pour the whole mixture into the saucepan. Mix thoroughly. Taste for seasoning, then heat on very low heat for 5 minutes before serving.

Serves 6–8

SOPA DE TORTILLA
TORTILLA SOUP

½ cup peanut, corn, or safflower oil
6 stale tortillas, cut in ½-inch strips
1 onion, chopped
2 cloves garlic, quartered
1 teaspoon dried *epazote*, crumbled
2 tomatoes, peeled, seeded, and chopped, or 3 canned Italian plum
    tomatoes, drained
6 cups chicken stock (homemade or canned)
1 tablespoon chopped coriander leaves
6 tablespoons grated Parmesan cheese

1. Heat the oil in a skillet and fry the tortilla strips till golden. Drain on paper toweling and set aside.
2. Pour off all but 2 tablespoons of oil from the skillet. Place the onion, garlic, *epazote,* and tomatoes in a blender or a food processor fitted with the steel blade. Purée until smooth; pour into the skillet and cook, uncovered, stirring occasionally, for about 5 minutes.
3. Bring the chicken stock to a boil in a large saucepan or soup pot. Add the cooked tomato mixture to the pot and reduce the heat to a simmer. Add the tortilla strips and simmer 5 minutes more. Sprinkle with coriander. Serve each portion with a tablespoon of grated Parmesan.

VARIATION: Fry 2 *chiles pasillas* in some of the oil in which the tortilla strips were fried. Allow to cool, then crumble. Serve a little along with the grated cheese, or on the side for those guests who like their tortilla soup a little *picante.*

Serves 6

SOPA DE LIMA
YUCATECAN LIME SOUP

THE SOUP:
    2 tablespoons peanut, corn, or safflower oil
    1 medium onion, finely chopped
    1 small green bell pepper, seeded, deveined, and chopped
    3 canned Italian plum tomatoes, drained and chopped
    8 cups chicken stock (homemade or canned)
    8 cloves garlic, finely minced
    ½ teaspoon dried oregano
    3 chicken gizzards
    6 chicken livers
    Salt and freshly ground pepper to taste
    1 whole chicken breast, boned and skinned
    ½ lime, plus 2 strips (about 1½×½ inches) lemon peel or grapefruit peel,
      minced

THE GARNISH:
  ¼ cup peanut, corn, or safflower oil
  6 or 8 stale tortillas, cut into thin strips
  ½ lime, chopped (including skin)
  1 small onion, finely chopped
  1 *chile serrano* (fresh or canned), finely chopped

  1. Heat 2 tablespoons oil in a skillet; add the onion and green pepper and sauté until the onion is translucent. Add the tomatoes; stir and crush with the back of a spoon. Set aside.
  2. Heat the chicken stock in a large saucepan or soup pot and add the garlic, oregano, gizzards, livers, salt, and pepper. Bring to a boil and simmer for 10 minutes. Add the chicken breast and continue cooking 15 minutes more.
  3. Remove the gizzards, livers, and breast to a chopping board and chop into small pieces. Return to the broth.
  4. Squeeze the juice of ½ lime into the broth and add the tomato-onion mixture, along with the lemon or grapefruit peel. Cook 5 minutes. Adjust the seasoning.
  5. Heat ¼ cup oil in a skillet and fry the tortilla strips. Drain on paper toweling. While still hot, place a few tortilla strips in each soup bowl. Ladle the soup over and serve with chopped onion, chopped chili, and chopped lime on the side. Have a pepper mill close at hand.

Serves 6

SOPA DE FRIJOL
BEAN SOUP

  1 cup dried beans (black, pink, red, or pinto)
  4 cups water
  4 cups chicken stock (homemade or canned)
  ¼ cup peanut, corn, or safflower oil
  2 medium onions, chopped
  4 cloves garlic, chopped
  ½ teaspoon crumbled *chile pequin*, or ¼ teaspoon cayenne pepper
  4 canned Italian plum tomatoes, drained and crushed
  ½ teaspoon dried oregano
  Salt and freshly ground pepper to taste
  ½ cup dry sherry
  ¼ cup grated Monterey Jack or Parmesan cheese

  1. Wash the beans and pick out any debris. Place them in a large saucepan or soup pot with the water and chicken stock; cover and simmer until almost tender (about 1½ hours).
  2. Heat the oil in a skillet and sauté the onions, garlic, and chili or cayenne until the onion is deep golden in color. Stir in the tomatoes, breaking them up as you do so. Heat through.
  3. Pour the onion mixture into the beans (undrained) along with the oregano, salt, and pepper. Simmer, covered, until the beans become very tender.

4. Remove the beans with a slotted spoon and purée them in a food processor fitted with the steel blade. Return the purée to the pot; stir in the sherry. Simmer a few minutes longer; mix the cheese into the soup and serve.

VARIATIONS: Sprinkle the soup with 2 or 3 corn tortillas—cut into 1-inch squares and fried crisp and golden in about ¼ cup oil. Fried tortilla bits can also be passed at the table.

Sprinkle each bowl generously with chopped scallions (both green and white parts of 2 stalks). Add lemon slices for additional taste and garnish.

Serves 6

SOPA POBLANA
A SOUP FROM PUEBLA

2 tablespoons peanut, corn, or safflower oil
½ pound boneless loin of pork, cut into small (½-inch) cubes
1 large onion, chopped
1 can (12 ounces) Green Giant Corn Niblets, drained well
3 small zucchini, halved lengthwise and cut in ¼-inch slices
2 small carrots, scraped and diced
2 fresh *chiles poblanos* (California, Anaheim, or Güero), roasted, peeled, seeded, deveined, and diced
4 canned Italian plum tomatoes, drained and puréed in blender or food processor
8 cups chicken stock (homemade or canned)
Salt and freshly ground pepper to taste
1 large ripe avocado, peeled and cubed
½ cup grated white cheddar or Monterey Jack cheese

1. Heat the oil in a large sauté pan. Add the pork cubes and sauté, stirring until the meat begins to brown. Cover and cook for 15 minutes over medium heat.
2. Add the onion, corn, zucchini, carrots, and chilies to the pork and stir for a few minutes until the onion starts to wilt.
3. Pour the tomato purée and chicken stock into the mixture; add salt and pepper. Simmer, covered, until vegetables are al dente, just barely tender. Serve with the avocado and cheese on the side.

Serves 6–8

POZOLE
PORK, CHICKEN, AND HOMINY SOUP

We call this a soup but it's really a one-dish meal. Originally made with a pig's head or pig's feet, it is just as delicious made with a lean cut of pork.

THE SOUP:
- 1½ pounds boneless pork loin or lean boneless pork shoulder, cut in 1-inch cubes
- 6 cups chicken stock (homemade or canned)
- 1 whole head garlic, peeled
- 1 large onion, coarsely chopped
- 1 teaspoon or more salt
- 1 teaspoon freshly ground pepper
- 1 chicken (3½ to 4 pounds) cut into serving pieces (or 6 chicken thighs; or 3 breasts, bone in, cut in half through the breastbone)
- 1 can (30 ounces) white hominy, drained

THE GARNISH:
- 3 *chiles serranos* or dried red chilies, crumbled
- 12 to 16 lime wedges
- 8 radishes, thinly sliced
- 1 head iceberg lettuce, chopped
- ½ cup finely chopped onion or 3 scallions, with greens, chopped
- 2 tablespoons dried oregano

1. Place the pork, along with the stock, garlic, onion, salt, and pepper in a soup pot and bring to a boil. Continue cooking for 15 minutes, skimming scum and foam from the surface if you like.

2. Add the chicken pieces to the stock and continue cooking another 30 to 45 minutes, skimming as necessary.

3. Add the hominy; bring to a boil again. Reduce the heat and simmer 15 minutes.

4. Taste and adjust seasoning; the soup will probably need more salt. Serve the broth, hominy, and meats together in deep bowls. Pass the garnishes (to be added to taste).

NOTE: For easier eating at the table, remove the skin and bones from the chicken, cut the chicken meat into bite-size pieces, and return to the broth before adding the hominy.

Serves 6–8

SOPAS SECAS: DRY SOUPS

The misnamed "dry soup" of Mexico is not soup at all, but a separate course very much like the risotto and pasta dishes of Italy. *Sopas secas* are usually listed as *sopas* on a Mexican restaurant menu, but they are meant to be chewed, not sipped. *Sopa de arroz*, for example, is not liquid soup made with rice; it is a rice dish often flecked with bits of chicken, pork, sausage, peas, carrots, tomatoes, and other vegetables. Pasta dishes, as well, will be listed as *sopas*. *Sopas secas* are usually served after a "wet" soup or first course at the big midday meal. In the United States, they can be the main course on a luncheon or supper menu—just as pasta might be—or a first course at a more elaborate dinner.

The Mexican method of cooking rice is quite similar to the European technique. Rice is sautéed in oil until it is a light golden color before the liquid is added. The flavor is even better when onions and garlic are sautéed in the oil before adding the rice. Seasonings may also be added to the oil before sautéeing. Rice cooked this way is extremely flavorful, served with fresh tortillas, a *picante* sauce, or all by itself. Topped with a fried egg, a rice dish makes an unusual brunch dish.

HOW TO COOK RICE (ARROZ BLANCO)

1. Make sure to use only long-grain rice, *not* converted rice or instant rice.
2. Traditionally, Mexican cooks rinse rice, but it isn't necessary. The rinsing process takes an hour or more. Unrinsed rice—straight from the box—produces a slightly starchier end product, but the difference is hardly noticeable. Besides being easier to use, unrinsed rice has the advantage of having more nutrients than rinsed rice, and reduces the chance of splattering when frying. But if you want to be perfectly authentic, place the rice in a bowl and cover it with very hot water. Let it stand to cool a little, then rub it, running it through your fingers, until the water is milky. Drain in a colander or a sieve and run under cold water. Rub and mix again with your fingers while the water runs, then allow the rice to stand in the colander or sieve until dry (shake the utensil several times during the drying process to release as much water as possible).
3. Sauté the raw rice in peanut, corn, or safflower oil. If you want the rice richer tasting and don't mind the cholesterol, use butter or lard. In either case, heat the indicated amount of oil in a heavy pot with a tight-fitting lid. Pour the rice into the pot and sauté it, mixing with a wooden spoon, until all the kernels are coated with oil and turn a golden color. At this point you can add onions and garlic and cook until they are limp. (Rice tastes livelier when the onions and garlic are sautéed in the oil until they take on a little color *before* the rice is added. Before adding the rice, you may also sauté meat, chicken livers, vegetables, etc., after cooking the onions and garlic. Seasonings, too, may be added at this point, followed by the rice and the liquid.)
4. To 1 cup of rice add 2 cups of hot liquid. (The liquid used in Mexico is often plain tap water. You might prefer homemade or canned chicken or

beef broth heated to boiling.) When using a tomato sauce or puréed tomatoes, measure them as part of the cooking liquid unless the recipe specifies otherwise. Boil the hot liquid with the rice for 3 or 4 minutes, stirring a few times. Turn the heat down to simmering and place the lid on the pot. Cook for about 20 minutes, or until the rice has absorbed all the liquid.

ARROZ A LA MEXICANA
MEXICAN STYLE RICE

¼ cup peanut, corn, or safflower oil or 4 tablespoons butter plus 2
 tablespoons oil
1 large (or two medium) onions, finely chopped
4 cloves garlic, thinly sliced
Salt and freshly ground pepper to taste
2 cups long-grain rice (unconverted)
4 cups chicken stock (homemade or canned)
1½ cups fresh, ripe, peeled, seeded, and chopped tomatoes or 1½ cups
 canned Italian tomatoes, chopped and puréed
½ box frozen green peas, thawed
Parsley or coriander sprigs for garnish

1. Heat the oil in a heavy saucepan with a tight-fitting lid. Add the onions, garlic, salt, and pepper and sauté until the onions are translucent and limp.

2. Add the rice to the oil; mix and sauté until all the grains are coated with oil and turn golden.

3. Bring the stock to a boil in another saucepan and add to the rice, along with the puréed tomatoes. Bring to a boil again. Lower the heat to simmering, cover, and cook until almost all the liquid has been absorbed (about 18 to 20 minutes).

4. Place the peas over the rice; cover and continue cooking for 5 minutes more, or until all the liquid has been absorbed. Mix the peas through and serve garnished with parsley or coriander sprigs.

VARIATION: For Arroz Amarillo (Yellow Rice), follow the recipe for Arroz a
 la Mexicana, omitting the peas.

Serves 6–8

ARROZ DE ORO
GOLDEN RICE

¼ cup peanut, corn, or safflower oil or 4 tablespoons butter plus 2
 tablespoons oil
2 tablespoons achiote (annatto) seeds
1 medium onion, finely chopped
2 cloves garlic, thinly sliced

2 cups long-grain rice (unconverted)
Salt and freshly ground pepper to taste
2 cups chicken stock (homemade or canned)
2 cups water

1. Heat the oil in a heavy saucepan with a tight-fitting lid. Add the annatto seeds and sauté over low heat until the oil is orange-red in color. Remove the seeds with a slotted spoon and discard.

2. Add the onion and garlic to the oil and sauté over high heat until limp and translucent. Add the rice, salt, and pepper; mix and sauté until all the grains are well coated with oil. Sauté 3 minutes longer.

4. Bring stock and water to a boil in another saucepan and pour over the rice; bring to a boil again; reduce the heat to simmering; cover and cook until all the liquid has been absorbed (about 20 minutes). The rice will be a lovely deep yellow.

Serves 6–8

ARROZ VERDE I
GREEN RICE

4 fresh *chiles poblanos* (California, Anaheim, or *Güero*), peeled, seeded,
   and deveined (page 17)
1 bunch parsley
3 sprigs coriander
1 large onion (or 2 medium), roughly chopped
2 cloves garlic, quartered
¼ cup peanut, corn, or safflower oil or 4 tablespoons butter plus 2
   tablespoons oil
2 cups long-grain rice (unconverted)
4 cups chicken stock (homemade or canned)
Salt and freshly ground pepper to taste

1. Place the chilies, parsley, coriander, onion, and garlic in the workbowl of a food processor fitted with the steel blade. Pulse several times, then process to a smooth purée.

2. Heat the oil in a heavy saucepan with a tight-fitting lid. Add the rice; mix and sauté until all the grains are well coated with oil. Add the purée to the oil and sauté further, scraping and mixing until the mixture is almost dry.

3. Add the stock, salt, and pepper to the pot and bring to a boil. Reduce the heat to simmering; cover and cook until all the liquid has been absorbed (about 20 minutes).

Serves 6–8

ARROZ VERDE II
GREEN RICE

1 can (10 ounces) Mexican green tomatoes, drained
¼ cup parsley leaves plus chopped parsley for garnish
1 clove garlic
1 large *chile poblano* (fresh or canned), cut in strips
2 tablespoons butter
1 small onion, chopped
2 cups long-grain rice (unconverted)
4 cups chicken stock (homemade or canned)
2 teaspoons cumin
Salt and freshly ground pepper to taste
1 bay leaf

1. Place the green tomatoes in a blender or workbowl of a food processor fitted with the steel blade; add the parsley, garlic, and chili. Blend or process for a few seconds until puréed.

2. Melt the butter in a small saucepan; add the chopped onion and sauté, stirring until the onion is wilted and well coated with butter. Add the rice to the saucepan; mix and sauté for several minutes until the rice turns golden. Add the puréed mixture to the rice and cook over medium heat for 5 minutes.

3. Add the chicken stock, cumin, salt, pepper, and bay leaf. Bring to a boil. Cover and lower the heat to simmering; cook for about 20 minutes, until the liquid is absorbed. Discard the bay leaf. Serve with additional chopped parsley.

NOTE: Green rice is lovely with grilled fish or meat, or with a simple stew. It can be turned into a main dish by adding 1 pound of scallops or shrimp (or a combination of both) 5 minutes before the rice is finished cooking.

Serves 6–8

SOPA SECA DE FIDEOS CON CHORIZOS Y CREMA
DRY PASTA SOUP WITH SAUSAGE AND SOUR CREAM

2 tablespoons peanut, corn, or safflower oil
2 chorizo sausages, casings removed, chopped
1 package (8 ounces) of vermicelli, linguine, or thin spaghetti
1 large onion (or 2 medium), roughly chopped
2 large cloves garlic, quartered
1 *chile ancho*, prepared as explained on page 16
2½ cups canned Italian plum tomatoes, chopped
½ teaspoon dried oregano
Salt and freshly ground pepper to taste
1 cup chicken stock (homemade or canned)
½ generous cup sour cream or *crème fraîche*

¼ cup grated Parmesan, mild cheddar, or Monterey Jack cheese
1 canned *chile chipotle,* drained and chopped

1. Heat the oil in a skillet and fry the sausages until browned. Remove with a slotted spoon and drain on paper towels.

2. Break the pasta in half and sauté quickly in the same oil until golden (stir constantly to prevent burning). Remove the pasta with tongs or a slotted spoon. Drain briefly on paper toweling and place in a flameproof casserole with cover.

3. Combine the onion, garlic, *chile ancho,* tomatoes, oregano, salt, and pepper in the workbowl of a food processor fitted with the steel blade and process to a smooth purée, stopping the processor once to scrape down the sides of the bowl with a spatula. Pour the purée into the heated oil left in the skillet in which the sausage and pasta were sautéed. Cook for 5 minutes, stirring; add the stock and bring to a boil.

4. Pour the purée over the pasta; cover, and cook over medium to low heat for 5 minutes; uncover; arrange sausage pieces on top; cover and cook about 5 minutes longer, or until the liquid has been absorbed.

5. Remove the casserole from the heat and spread the sour cream over the sausages and pasta; sprinkle with grated cheese and run under the broiler until the cheese melts and the cream just begins to bubble. Sprinkle with chopped chile chipotle.

VARIATIONS: 1. Follow the above recipe, leaving out the chorizos and sour cream. Serve with extra cheese at table.

2. Instead of sausages, spread the pasta with a layer of leftover Picadillo (page 76).

3. Instead of sausages, sprinkle the pasta with slivers of cooked chicken.

4. Replace the sausages with 3 eggs, scrambled with canned chopped green chilies and well seasoned with red pepper flakes.

Serves 4 as a main course,
or 6 as a first course

FIDEOS CON "PESTO"
PASTA WITH MEXICAN PESTO SAUCE

An Italian friend living in Mexico City improvised with local ingredients to come up with a Mexican-Italian Pesto.

1 bunch coriander
1 bunch parsley
½ cup walnut meats or pine nuts
6 cloves garlic, quartered
1 cup light Italian olive oil
Salt and freshly ground pepper to taste
1 cup grated Parmesan cheese plus extra for garnish
1 pound vermicelli, linguine, or thin spaghetti

1. Place all the ingredients (except the pasta) in the workbowl of a food processor fitted with the steel blade. Pulse several times. Scrape down the sides of the bowl with a spatula and pulse a few more times until the mixture is finely chopped but not puréed.

2. Drop the pasta into 4 quarts of rapidly boiling water. Stir several times and bring to a boil, uncovered. Cook at a boil for 8 minutes, stirring once or twice. Taste a strand to see if it is done (tender but chewy).

3. Drain the pasta in a colander; transfer to a serving bowl. Spoon the pesto in to taste and toss to mix thoroughly. Pass more sauce at the table along with extra grated Parmesan.

Serves 4–6

FIDEOS CON SALSA DE ALMENDRA VERDE
FETTUCINE WITH GREEN ALMOND SAUCE

2¼ cups Salsa Almendra Verde (page 37), made with Parmesan cheese
½ cup heavy cream, sour cream, or *crème fraîche*
1 pound fresh fettucine or egg noodles
Grated Parmesan cheese

1. In a large sauté pan over low heat, heat Salsa Almendra Verde. Add the heavy cream and heat through, but do not boil.

2. Drop the fresh fettucine into 4 quarts of rapidly boiling salted water; cover and bring to a boil again. Take off the heat immediately (fresh pasta cooks very quickly and it will be cooked further when combined with the sauce). Drain the pasta in a colander and transfer to the pan containing the hot sauce.

3. Toss pasta and sauce thoroughly over medium to low heat until the noodles are coated completely. Serve immediately, and pass extra grated Parmesan at the table.

Serves 4

FIDEOS PARAÍSO
HEAVENLY FETTUCINE

½ pound chorizo sausages, casings removed
1 tablespoon oil
3 tablespoons butter
1 clove garlic, finely chopped
½ pound mushrooms, sliced
½ pound fresh spinach leaves, washed, drained, and chopped
1 cup heavy cream, sour cream, or *crème fraîche*
1 pound fresh fettucine or egg noodles
⅔ cup freshly grated Parmesan cheese plus extra for garnish
1 teaspoon freshly ground pepper
Pinch of ground allspice

1. Heat a heavy skillet or sauté pan large enough to hold all the ingredients comfortably. Break up the chorizos and fry them in very little oil until nicely browned. Remove with a slotted spoon and set aside.

2. Bring 4 quarts of salted water to a rapid boil.

3. Pour off any fat from the pan. Return the pan to medium heat and melt the butter. Add the garlic and sauté until golden. Add the mushrooms and cook until their moisture evaporates. Add the spinach leaves and stir until wilted. Add the cream and heat through, but do not boil. Turn off the heat.

4. Drop the fettucine into the boiling water; cover the pot and return to a boil. Drain immediately in a colander and transfer to the pan containing the cream mixture. Turn the heat to low and toss the fettucine with sauce to coat. Add ⅔ cup grated cheese, pepper, and allspice and toss again. Serve immediately with more grated cheese passed at the table.

Serves 4

SOPA SECA DE TORTILLA CON PICADILLO
DRY SOUP OF TORTILLAS WITH PICADILLO

4 tablespoons peanut, corn, or safflower oil
2 medium onions, thinly sliced
4 cloves garlic, chopped
½ pound ground pork
½ pound lean ground beef
1 pound fresh, ripe tomatoes, seeded, peeled, and chopped, or 6 canned
    Italian plum tomatoes, drained and chopped
Salt and freshly ground pepper to taste
1 scant teaspoon dried oregano
½ teaspoon ground cumin
1 *chile jalapeño* (fresh or canned), seeded, deveined, and chopped
10 6-inch, day-old tortillas, cut into ½-inch strips
½ cup sour cream, *crème fraîche,* or heavy cream
½ cup grated Parmesan, Monterey Jack, or Havarti cheese

1. Heat 2 tablespoons of the oil in a heavy skillet or sauté pan and sauté the onions and garlic until golden. Add the pork and beef and cook, stir-

ring until all the bits are browned. Add the tomatoes, salt and pepper, oregano, cumin, and chili and cook a few minutes longer. Set the mixture aside.

2. Heat the remaining oil in the skillet over high heat and fry the tortilla strips without allowing them to become too crisp or browned. Remove to paper toweling to drain.

3. Preheat the oven to 350°F. Spread a layer of the meat and tomato mixture in a shallow, ovenproof casserole, then add a layer of tortilla strips; repeat until all the ingredients are used, ending with a layer of tortilla strips. Spread the top layer with cream and sprinkle with cheese. Place, uncovered, in the preheated oven for about 30 minutes, or until heated through and bubbly.

Serves 4–6

SOPA SECA DE TORTILLA CON POLLO Y HIGADO DE POLLO
DRY SOUP OF TORTILLAS WITH CHICKEN AND CHICKEN LIVERS

5 tablespoons peanut, corn, or safflower oil
2 medium onions, thinly sliced
4 cloves garlic, chopped
½ pound chicken livers
1 can (10 ounces) Mexican green tomatoes, drained
1 *chile jalapeño* or *serrano* (fresh or canned), seeded, deveined, and chopped
Salt and freshly ground pepper to taste
2 tablespoons chopped coriander leaves
1 whole chicken breast, skinned and boned, cut into bite-size chunks
10 6-inch, day-old tortillas, cut into ½-inch strips
½ cup sour cream or *crème fraîche*
½ cup chopped scallions, with greens

1. Heat 2 tablespoons of the oil in a heavy skillet or sauté pan and sauté the onions and garlic until lightly browned. Add the chicken livers and sauté until browned, stirring to break the livers up into small pieces. Add the green tomatoes, chili, salt, pepper, and coriander leaves and simmer for 5 minutes, stirring and scraping up the browned bits clinging to the pan. When done, pour into a bowl and set aside.

2. In the same pan, sauté the chicken breasts in 1 tablespoon of the oil until just cooked through (about 2 or 3 minutes). Lift out and set aside.

3. Heat the remaining oil in the pan and fry the tortilla strips without allowing them to become too crisp or brown. Remove to paper towels to drain.

4. Preheat the oven to 350°F. Spread half the liver and tomato mixture in a shallow, ovenproof casserole. Arrange a layer of half the chicken on top, then a layer of half the tortilla strips on top of that. Repeat the layers, ending with tortilla strips. Spread the top layer with sour cream and heat in the oven for 20 minutes. Sprinkle the top with chopped scallions before serving.

Serves 4–6

PUDÍN AZTECA
AZTEC PUDDING

2 whole chicken breasts, bone in
4 fresh *chiles poblanos* (California, Anaheim, or Güero), skinned, seeded,
    and deveined as explained on page 17
2 tablespoons peanut, corn, or safflower oil
1½ pounds fresh, ripe tomatoes, peeled, seeded, and puréed, or ½ can (28-
    ounce size) Italian tomato purée
2 medium onions, finely chopped
Salt and freshly ground pepper to taste
4 eggs, separated
Oil for skillet
8 tortillas
2 cups grated Monterey Jack or Havarti cheese

1. Place the chicken breasts in salted water to cover and poach until tender
(about 45 minutes); cool in the broth, then skin, bone, and shred with two
forks or cut into narrow strips. Set aside.
2. Cut the chilies into narrow strips and set aside.
3. Preheat oven to 350°F.
4. Heat 2 tablespoons oil in a heavy skillet or sauté pan and cook the onions until translucent. Add the puréed tomatoes and simmer, stirring, for
about 5 minutes, until slightly thickened. Salt and pepper to taste and set
aside.
5. Beat the egg yolks with a fork until slightly frothy. Beat the whites until stiff and fold in the beaten yolks a little at a time.
6. Heat ¼ inch of oil in a heavy skillet until it begins to smoke. Dip a tortilla in the egg mixture to coat both sides and fry in the hot oil until golden
brown. Place the tortilla in a round casserole or soufflé dish and sprinkle
with chilies, chicken, a heaping spoonful of sauce, and some of the cheese.
Dip and fry another tortilla. Place it on top of the tortilla in the casserole
and top with filling; repeat until all the tortillas and filling are used. Try to
end with a tortilla on top. If there is any egg remaining, pour it over the top.
Place the casserole in the oven and cook until browned, about 20 minutes.

Serves 4 generously

CHILAQUILES
TORTILLA CASSEROLE

16 stale corn tortillas
Peanut, corn, or safflower oil for frying (½ inch)
1 can (10 ounces) Mexican green tomatoes, drained
3 *chiles serranos* (fresh or canned), seeded and deveined
1 teaspoon dried *epazote*, crumbled (optional)

3 sprigs coriander
2 medium onions, chopped
1 cup grated Parmesan or Monterey Jack cheese
1 cup hot chicken stock (homemade or canned)
4 radishes, sliced
1 tablespoon chopped coriander leaves

1. Cut the tortillas into ½-inch wide strips. Heat the oil in a heavy skillet or sauté pan and fry the strips until golden but not brown or crisp. Remove and drain on paper toweling.

2. Purée the green tomatoes, chilies, *epazote*, coriander, and half the chopped onions in a blender or food processor fitted with the steel blade.

3. Pour the oil out of the skillet used to fry the tortilla strips, allowing the oil that clings to the bottom to remain. Heat this oil; pour in the purée and cook for 3 or 4 minutes over high heat, stirring.

4. Grease a flameproof casserole and layer the bottom with half the tortilla strips. Sprinkle with half the cheese. Cover the cheese with half the remaining onions. Spoon half the green tomato sauce over the onions. Repeat the layers and pour the hot chicken stock over all. Cook over low heat until the tortilla strips are quite soft and the cheese is melted. Serve immediately, garnished with radish slices and the chopped coriander (these may be passed at the table, if you'd like).

Serves 4

CHILAQUILES ESTILO SEÑOR GERALDO
JERRY'S TORTILLA CASSEROLE

1 pound fresh, ripe tomatoes, peeled, seeded, and chopped, or 6 canned
    Italian plum tomatoes, drained and chopped
3 *chiles serranos* or *jalapeños* (fresh or canned), seeded, deveined, and
    chopped
10 stale corn tortillas
4 tablespoons butter
Salt and freshly ground pepper to taste
½ cup sour cream or *crème fraîche*
½ cup grated Monterey Jack or mild white cheddar

1. Purée the tomatoes and chilies in the workbowl of a food processor fitted with the steel blade or in a blender.

2. Cut the tortillas into quarters. Melt the butter in a heavy skillet or sauté pan and cook the tortilla quarters until crisp and golden (not brown). Add the tomato-chili mixture to the pan with the tortilla pieces and simmer for 5 minutes, or until the tortilla quarters begin to soften slightly. Season with salt and pepper to taste. Spread with the sour cream and sprinkle with the cheese. Serve immediately, or run under the broiler first to melt the cheese.

Serves 4

CARNES: MEATS

Pork, introduced to Mexico by Cortes's soldiers, is the favored meat of Mexican cooks. There are many innovative and amusingly titled pork dishes, such as "pork tablecloth stainer," "pork in confetti" (with red, yellow, and green diced peppers), and "pork dressed in satin" (with a smooth-as-silk nut purée). Beef, introduced to Mexico along with lamb well after the Conquest, has a less enthusiastic following, yet has inspired some delicious recipes. Veal is used as rarely in Mexico as it is here, mainly because of its high price. Still, there are a host of exquisitely subtle veal preparations in the Mexican repertoire. Brains, tripe, liver, and other organ meats are used extensively—especially tongue, which has a versatile and varied group of recipes to its credit.

A few of our favorites may take a little longer to produce, but they are quick to assemble and need no watching while they cook. Made ahead of time (put up on a weekend, for instance), they need only to be heated through just before serving.

PICADILLO

5 tablespoons peanut, corn, or safflower oil
4 onions, coarsely cut
6 cloves garlic, chopped
Salt and freshly ground pepper to taste
2 pounds chopped very lean beef or 1 pound chopped beef plus 1 pound chopped pork (lean shoulder or butt)
1 pound fresh, ripe tomatoes, peeled, seeded, and chopped, or 1 can (35 ounces) Italian plum tomatoes, drained and crushed
3 canned *chiles jalapeños*, seeded and sliced into rings or chopped
1 can (4 ounces) green chilies, drained
2 pieces (4×1 inches) pieces zest from an orange, diced in small pieces or very thinly julienned (use a swivel-head potato peeler to remove zest only, without pith)
½ cup raisins (optional)
½ teaspoon ground cinnamon
½ teaspoon ground cloves
½ teaspoon ground allspice
½ teaspoon grated nutmeg
2 large tart apples, cored, pared, and cubed
¼ cup pitted green olives or pimiento-stuffed green olives, sliced
¼ cup slivered almonds

1. Heat 4 tablespoons of the oil in a large, heavy sauté pan; add the onions, garlic, salt, and pepper and fry until the onions are lightly golden. Add the meat and stir until all the bits are browned. Stir in the tomatoes, chilies, orange zest, raisins, cinnamon, cloves, allspice, and nutmeg and simmer, uncovered, 20 to 30 minutes.

2. Ten minutes before serving, mix in the apples and green olives and heat through. (The apples should not become mushy.)

3. In a small skillet, fry the almonds in the remaining 1 tablespoon oil until they are golden.

4. Spoon the picadillo into a deep serving dish or casserole and sprinkle the almonds over the top.

VARIATIONS: Add or substitute firm-textured pears, pineapple, bananas, or other seasonal fresh fruits. Just be sure they are not cooked too long, or they will disintegrate or lose their texture. Jícama, diced, is also nice and crunchy.

Instead of fruit, use 2 Idaho potatoes, pared and diced in ½-inch pieces and add with the tomatoes.

Substitute 1 teaspoon ground cumin for the ½ teaspoon allspice, or add it in addition to the allspice.

Picadillo is also delicious when you substitute 1 teaspoon dried oregano and ½ teaspoon dried thyme for the spices.

Try soaking the raisins in ½ cup dry sherry, then heat the sherry in a small saucepan; ignite, when the flame dies, add the raisins and sherry to the picadillo.

Substitute capers for the olives and add with the fruit.

Serves 6

CASUELA DE TORTILLA Y POLLO Y TOMATES VERDES
CASSEROLE OF TORTILLAS, CHICKEN, AND GREEN TOMATOES

THE SAUCE:
2½ cups sour cream or *crème fraîche*
1 medium onion, finely chopped
½ cup finely chopped coriander leaves
4 cloves garlic, minced
Salt and freshly ground pepper to taste
3 cups Salsa Verde (page 33)

THE CHICKEN:
2 tablespoons peanut, corn, or safflower oil
1 medium onion, chopped
4 cloves garlic, minced
1 large or 2 small chicken breasts, skinned and boned (about 1½ pounds)
Salt and freshly ground pepper to taste

THE TORTILLAS:
½ cup peanut, corn, or safflower oil
18 tortillas
2 cups grated Parmesan, white cheddar, or Monterey Jack cheese

1. Combine the sour cream with the rest of the sauce ingredients in a mixing bowl. Refrigerate until ready to assemble the casserole.

2. Heat 2 tablespoons oil in a skillet or sauté pan and fry the onion and garlic until golden; add salt and pepper and the chicken breasts. Turn the heat to medium and sauté the chicken until just cooked through.

3. Remove the breasts from the skillet. With two forks, pull the meat apart, into shreds.

4. Return the chicken shreds to the skillet and mix with the onions and garlic. Turn off the heat.

5. When you are ready to assemble the casserole, heat ½ cup oil to smoking in a heavy skillet and cook the tortillas a few seconds on each side. Do *not* cook until crisp. Drain on paper toweling.

6. Preheat the oven to 350°F.

7. In a rectangular baking dish (about 13×9×2 inches), overlap 6 still-warm tortillas, then add half the chicken mixture, then one-third of the cheese. Repeat with 6 more tortillas to cover the bottom; ladle about one-third of the *salsa verde*–sour cream sauce over the tortillas, half the remaining sauce, the remaining chicken, and half the remaining cheese. Repeat again, this time using the remaining 6 tortillas, remaining sauce, and remaining cheese. Cover tightly with aluminum foil and bake the casserole, for 30 to 40 minutes.

8. Five minutes before serving, remove the foil and run the dish under broiler to turn the cheese golden and crusty.

TO PREPARE AHEAD: The casserole may be refrigerated until 1 hour before baking time, or it may be frozen for later use. (Defrost for several hours before baking.)

Serves 6

CHILES RELLENOS
CHILIES STUFFED WITH PICADILLO

6 fresh *chiles poblanos* (or large California or Anaheim) or, if unavailable,
  6 green bell peppers
½ recipe Picadillo (page 76)
1 pound fresh, ripe tomatoes (about 3), peeled, seeded, and chopped, or 1
  can (16 ounces) Italian plum tomatoes, drained and chopped
1 medium onion, chopped
3 cloves garlic, quartered
Peanut, corn, or safflower oil
1 cup chicken stock (homemade or canned)
Pinch of dried thyme
Salt and freshly ground pepper to taste
2 eggs, separated
½ cup all-purpose flour

1. Impale a chili on a fork and hold it over a gas flame or electric burner until the skin blackens and blisters. Repeat with each chili. Place the chilies in a damp cloth or in a plastic storage bag or brown paper bag; close the

bag and let the chilies cool for 30 minutes. Peel the chilies; the thin skin should come off easily.

2. When skinned, slit each chili lengthwise and remove stem, seeds, and veins. (If using bell peppers, cut out the stem ends, remove seeds and veins, and save the stems to plug up the ends after stuffing. Taste a tiny bit of a chili. If too hot, soak in salted water for a few hours before stuffing.

3. Cook the prepared chilies in boiling water for 5 minutes. Drain well.

4. Stuff the chilies with the *picadillo* and set aside.

5. Combine the tomatoes, onion, and garlic in the workbowl of a food processor fitted with the steel blade and purée until smooth, adding a little of the stock if necessary.

6. Heat 1 tablespoon oil in a saucepan or sauté pan large enough to hold the chilies and add the purée. Cook, stirring, for about 5 minutes. Mix in the stock and season with salt, pepper, and thyme. Simmer for a few minutes. Set aside.

7. Beat the egg yolks well. Beat the whites until they are glossy and hold stiff peaks. Fold the whites into the yolks.

8. Heat the oil in a deep fryer or saucepan to between 360° and 375°F on a deep-fry thermometer.

9. Dip the chilies in flour, coating them well, then dip them in the egg. Fry in the hot oil until golden brown. Drain on paper toweling for a few minutes.

10. Reheat the tomato sauce and arrange the chilies in the hot sauce. Cook for only 2 or 3 minutes on medium heat. Transfer the chilies to a warm serving dish and spoon the sauce over and around them.

Serves 6

CHILES RELLENOS DE FRIJOLES
CHILIES STUFFED WITH BEANS

6 *chiles poblanos* (California, Anaheim, or Güero), prepared as in Chiles Rellenos (page 17)
3 cups Frijoles Refritos (page 120)
2 eggs, separated
½ cup plus 2 tablespoons all-purpose flour
Peanut, corn, or safflower oil for frying
2 tablespoons butter
1 cup milk
½ cup heavy cream (or use all milk)
Salt and white pepper to taste
½ cup grated white cheddar or Monterey Jack cheese

1. Stuff the prepared chilies with the refried beans.

2. Beat the egg yolks well. Beat the whites until they are glossy and hold stiff peaks. Fold the whites into the yolks.

3. Heat the oil in a deep fryer or saucepan to between 360° and 375°F on a deep-fry thermometer.

4. Dip the stuffed chilies in the ½ cup flour, coating them well, then dip them in the egg. Fry in the hot oil until golden brown. Drain on paper toweling for a few minutes while you heat the oven and prepare the sauce.

5. Preheat the oven to 350°F.

6. Melt the butter in a saucepan. Stir in the 2 tablespoons flour. Gradually add the milk and cream. Stir until the sauce boils and thickens. Stir in salt and pepper to taste; add the cheese. Cook, stirring, until the cheese melts.

7. Arrange the stuffed chilies in an ovenproof baking dish and pour the cheese sauce over them. Bake, uncovered, for about 15 minutes.

VARIATIONS: After frying the stuffed chilies, arrange them on a serving platter; spoon sour cream or *crème fraîche* over the chilies and decorate with slivered blanched almonds, pomegranate seeds, or pumpkin seeds.

Serves 6

CHILES RELLENOS EN NOGADA
STUFFED CHILIES IN WALNUT SAUCE

Truly authentic *chiles rellenos en nogada* should be served decorated with the seeds of one small pomegranate and sprigs of Italian parsley sprinkled over the sauce. But a cook we know in Cuernavaca sprinkles 1 teaspoon chopped crystallized ginger over the sauce.

THE CHILIES:
Prepare 6 chilies as for Chiles Rellenos (page 78). Fry in batter as described and drain on paper toweling.

THE SAUCE:
½ cups walnuts, soaked in water overnight and drained
1 package (8 ounces) cream cheese or farmer cheese, chunked
1 cup sour cream or *crème fraîche*
¼ teaspoon ground cinnamon
¼ cup fine fresh bread crumbs
½ teaspoon sugar or ¼ teaspoon salt
Milk (optional)

1. In the workbowl of a food processor fitted with the steel blade, process all the ingredients (except the optional milk) to a smooth purée. The sauce should be the consistency of mayonnaise. If it is too thick, pulse a little milk into the sauce.

2. Arrange the warm *chiles rellenos* on a serving platter; pour the sauce over them and serve.

Serves 6

PUERCO EN ADOBO ROJO
PORK LOIN IN RED ADOBO SAUCE

Some Mexicans like their *adobo* sweeter than this recipe. If you want to go Mexican, add more sugar to taste.

THE PORK:
  3 to 4 pounds boneless pork loin, cut into 1½- to 2-inch cubes
  Salt and freshly ground pepper to taste
  1 whole onion stuck with 3 or 4 cloves
  2 cloves garlic, peeled

THE ADOBO:
  6 *chiles anchos*, prepared as directed on page 17
  1 medium to large onion, coarsely chopped
  8 cloves garlic, coarsely chopped
  ½ teaspoon dried oregano
  ½ teaspoon ground cumin
  ½ teaspoon cinnamon
  4 whole cloves (or ½ teaspoon ground cloves)
  ½ teaspoon ground allspice
  2 tablespoons mild white vinegar
  1 teaspoon sugar (or to taste)
  Freshly ground pepper to taste
  ½ teaspoon salt (or to taste)
  3 canned Italian plum tomatoes, drained and chopped
  1½ cups reserved stock from pork
  2 tablespoons lard (or fat rendered from pork loin trimmings) or 2
      tablespoons peanut, corn, or safflower oil

  1. Place the pork cubes, whole onion stuck with cloves, the garlic, salt, and pepper in enough water to cover. Bring the water to a boil, then simmer for 1 hour. Pour off the stock and reserve. Set the pork aside. Discard the onion and garlic.

  2. Put the prepared chilies, along with the rest of the *adobo* ingredients (except the pork stock and lard or oil), in the workbowl of a food processor fitted with the steel blade and process until smooth, adding a little pork stock if necessary.

  3. Heat the lard or oil in a large skillet or sauté pan and sauté the pork cubes lightly. Remove the pork from the pan and set aside.

  4. Pour the purée into the pan and cook for 5 minutes, stirring constantly. Thin the sauce with about 1 cup of the reserved pork stock.

  5. Add the cooked pork to the sauce and simmer, uncovered, for 30 minutes.

  6. Taste the sauce and adjust the seasonings. The sauce should be fairly thick so it coats the meat. If you like, serve with hot tortillas and Arroz Blanco (page 66).

SUGGESTION: You may garnish the *adobo* with thinly sliced raw onion. Also, any leftover sauce can be mixed with the sautéed ground meat or sausage as a filling for tacos. Or it can be mixed with lightly sautéed vegetables as a sauce or as a filling for eggs. The sauce may be made ahead and kept in the refrigerator for 2 or 3 days. It also freezes well.

Serves 6–8

PUERCO EN ADOBO VERDE
PORK LOIN IN GREEN ADOBO SAUCE

THE PORK:
  3 to 4 pounds boneless pork loin, cut into 1½- to 2-inch cubes
  Salt and freshly ground pepper to taste
  1 whole onion stuck with 3 or 4 cloves
  2 cloves garlic, peeled

THE ADOBO:
  3 *chiles anchos*, prepared as directed on page 16
  3 canned *chiles jalapeños*, seeded and chopped
  1 medium to large onion, coarsely chopped
  8 cloves garlic, coarsely chopped
  ½ teaspoon dried oregano
  ½ teaspoon ground cumin
  1 tablespoon mild white vinegar
  6 romaine lettuce leaves, chopped
  ½ can (10-ounce size) Mexican green tomatoes, with liquid
  3 tablespoons chopped coriander leaves
  2 tablespoons peanut, corn, or safflower oil
  ½ cup orange juice
  2 tablespoons chopped orange rind
  Salt and freshly ground pepper to taste

   1. Place the pork cubes, whole onion stuck with cloves, and garlic, salt and pepper in enough water to cover. Bring the water to a boil, then simmer for 1 hour. Pour off the stock and discard (or save for another use). Set the pork aside. Discard the onion and garlic.
   2. Put the prepared chilies, along with the rest of the *adobo* ingredients (except orange juice, rind, salt, and pepper), in the workbowl of a food processor fitted with the steel blade and process until smooth.
   3. Heat the oil in a large skillet or sauté pan and sauté the pork cubes lightly. Remove the pork from the pan and set aside.
   4. Pour the purée into the pan and cook for 5 minutes, stirring constantly. Add the cooked pork. Thin the sauce with the orange juice; add the orange rind, salt, and pepper and simmer, uncovered, for about 30 minutes. The sauce should be thick.

TO PREPARE AHEAD: The sauce can be made ahead of time and kept in the refrigerator for 2 or 3 days. It also freezes well.

Serves 6–8

LOMO DE CERDO EN NARANJA
PORK LOIN IN ORANGE SAUCE

THE MEAT:
3 pounds boneless pork loin
1 tablespoon ground cinnamon
½ teaspoon ground cloves
1 tablespoon ground coriander
Salt and freshly ground pepper to taste
3 tablespoons peanut, corn, or safflower oil

THE SAUCE:
1 large onion, coarsely chopped
6 cloves garlic, peeled
1 cup (or more) fresh orange juice
1 cup (or more) hot water
Peel of 2 oranges, cut in dice
¼ cup golden raisins, plumped in 2 tablespoons sweet sherry
2 tablespoons capers, drained
¼ cup slivered, blanched almonds
2 oranges, peeled, seeded, and sliced

1. Sprinkle the pork with the spices, salt, and pepper.
2. Heat the oil in a large skillet or sauté pan and brown the pork on all sides. Add the onion and garlic and sauté until the onion is translucent and tender. Add the orange juice, hot water, and diced peel. Cover and cook for 1½ hours or more, replenishing juice and water, if it cooks away. When the pork is tender, remove from the pan and slice into serving pieces.
3. Remove the garlic cloves from the skillet and mash with a fork. Return the pork and garlic to the sauce. Add more juice and water, if necessary, to make a least 1 cup of liquid. Add the raisins, with the sherry, and capers. Bring to a boil and cook for a few minutes to meld the flavors and reduce the sauce slightly. To serve, alternate pork slices and orange slices on a platter and sprinkle with almonds. Or arrange the pork slices on a platter, garnish with orange slices, and sprinkle with almonds.

Serves 6–8

COCHINITA PIBIL
YUCATECAN BARBECUED PORK

2 tablespoons achiote (annatto) seeds made into paste as directed on page 11
2 tablespoons mild white vinegar
¼ teaspoon ground cumin
1 teaspoon dried oregano
8 cloves garlic, peeled
1 tablespoon salt
1 teaspoon freshly ground pepper
4 pounds pork loin, bone in
2 medium to large onions, thinly sliced

1. Add the vinegar to the achiote paste and place in the workbowl of a food processor fitted with the steel blade, along with the cumin, oregano, garlic, salt, and pepper. Purée.

2. With a sharp knife, score the meat in a diamond pattern and spread with the purée. Allow to stand at room temperature for 2 hours.

3. Place the pork loin on a piece of aluminum foil large enough to wrap the meat completely; lay the onion slices over the meat and wrap tightly by folding the edges over each other so they are practically airtight.

4. Preheat the oven to 350°F.

5. Set the foil-wrapped meat on a rack in a covered roasting pan. Pour water into the pan to a depth of 1 or 2 inches; cover and bake for 4 to 5 hours. Check the pan every once in a while to be sure the water level is maintained and add boiling water if necessary. When done, the meat should be so tender it falls from the bone.

6. Unwrap and shred the meat at the table; roll into hot tortillas and serve with Salsa de Barbacoa (recipe follows).

Serves 6

SALSA DE BARBACOA
BARBECUE SAUCE

1 can (35 ounces) Italian plum tomatoes, drained
2 cloves garlic, quartered
1 medium onion, coarsely chopped
1 tablespoon chopped coriander leaves
2 canned *chiles serranos*, chopped
1 tablespoon light Italian olive oil
1 teaspoon salt (or to taste)

Purée all the ingredients in a blender or the workbowl of a food processor fitted with the steel blade. Taste; add more *chiles serranos* if you like a hotter sauce.

Makes about 3 cups

LOMO DE CERDO EN TOMATES VERDES
LOIN OF PORK IN GREEN TOMATO SAUCE

2 tablespoons peanut, corn, or safflower oil
1 large onion, finely chopped
3 cloves garlic, minced
3 pounds boneless pork loin, cut into 2-inch cubes
2 cans (10 ounces each) Mexican green tomatoes, puréed with their liquid in blender or food processor
3 tablespoons chopped fresh coriander
3 canned mild *chiles jalapeños*, drained and cut into strips
Salt and freshly ground pepper to taste

1. Heat the oil in a large casserole and sauté the onion and garlic until the onion is translucent. Add the pork cubes and brown on all sides. Add the puréed green tomatoes, coriander, and chilies. Season well with salt and pepper.

2. Cover and simmer over low heat until the pork is tender, about 2 hours.

Serves 6

JAMÓN ASADO EN SALSA VERDE CON CACAHUATES
ROAST FRESH HAM WITH GREEN PEANUT SAUCE

THE SAUCE:
  ½ cup dry-roasted peanuts
  1 can (10 ounces) Mexican green tomatoes, drained
  6 sprigs coriander
  ¼ teaspoon freshly ground pepper
  3 canned *chiles serranos*, drained and seeded
  3 cloves garlic, peeled
  ½ cup chicken stock (homemade or canned)

THE HAM:
  2 tablespoons peanut, corn, or safflower oil
  1 medium onion, thinly sliced
  2 pounds cooked fresh ham, cut in 1-inch cubes
  2 cups (or more) chicken stock (homemade or canned)
  Salt and freshly ground pepper to taste

1. Place the sauce ingredients in the workbowl of a food processor fitted with the steel blade and process to a smooth purée.

2. In a heavy skillet, heat the oil and sauté the onion until lightly browned; add the cooked ham and toss until the ham is heated through. Add the sauce and cook for 3 or 4 minutes, stirring and scraping all the while. Add 2 cups chicken stock; heat through and taste for seasoning. Simmer, uncovered, for 15 minutes longer, adding more stock if the sauce gets too thick (it should be slightly runny). Serve over white rice or noodles.

Serves 6

TERNERA CON ALPACARRAS
VEAL WITH CAPER SAUCE

THE VEAL:
  3 pounds boneless veal shoulder or veal breast
  1 medium onion, cut into eighths
  4 cloves garlic, halved
  1 teaspoon dried thyme
  1 bay leaf
  1 teaspoon salt

THE SAUCE:
  2 medium onions, chopped
  3 cloves garlic, chopped
  1 bottle capers, drained
  3 canned *chiles serranos*, drained and seeded
  3 fresh *chiles poblanos* (California or Anaheim), seeded, deveined, and
    cut in ½-inch strips
  1 can (16 ounces) Italian plum tomatoes, drained
  Salt and freshly ground pepper to taste
  2 tablespoons peanut, corn, or safflower oil

  1. Place the veal in a large saucepan with the onion, garlic, thyme, bay
leaf, and salt. Cover with water; bring to a boil. Reduce the heat and simmer uncovered, for 1 hour, or until tender. Skim every once in a while to
remove surface scum.
  2. Allow the veal to cool in its broth, then remove from the pan; strain and
reserve the broth. Cut the veal into 2-inch strips; set aside.
  3. Combine the chopped onions, garlic, half the capers, the canned and
fresh chilies, salt, and pepper, and some of the veal broth in the workbowl
of a food processor fitted with the steel blade. Process to a smooth purée,
adding more stock if necessary.
  4. Heat the oil in a large skillet or sauté pan. Add the purée and cook,
stirring, over moderate heat for a few minutes. Pour in only enough broth
to make the sauce the consistency of heavy cream. Adjust the seasoning. Add
the veal strips and simmer for 5 minutes to meld flavors and heat the veal.
Transfer to a warm serving platter and sprinkle with the remaining capers.

Serves 6

TERNERA EN NOGADA
VEAL IN WALNUT SAUCE

THE VEAL:
  3 pounds boneless veal shoulder or veal breast
  1 medium onion, cut into eighths
  4 garlic cloves, halved
  1 teaspoon dried thyme
  1 bay leaf
  1 teaspoon salt
  2 sprigs parsley

THE SAUCE:
  2 tablespoons butter
  2 medium onions, chopped
  1¼ cups walnuts, ground
  1 cup heavy cream
  Reserved broth from veal
  Salt and freshly ground pepper to taste
  ½ cup sour cream or *crème fraîche*
  ¼ cup toasted, slivered almonds or the seeds from a small pomegranate

1. Place the veal in a large saucepan with the onion, garlic, thyme, bay leaf, salt, and parsley. Cover with water; bring to a boil. Reduce the heat and simmer, uncovered, for 1 hour, or until tender. Skim occasionally to remove surface scum.

2. Allow the veal to cool in its broth, then remove from the pan, strain and reserve the broth. Cut the veal into 2-inch strips; set aside.

3. In a large skillet or sauté pan, heat the butter and sauté the chopped onions until soft and golden. Add the walnuts, heavy cream, reserved broth, salt, and pepper and simmer until the sauce is slightly thickened. Add the veal and simmer 5 minutes more. Add the sour cream; stir until blended and heated through. Transfer to a warm serving platter and sprinkle with almonds or pomegranate seeds.

Serves 6

CARNE EN TOMATES VERDES
BEEF WITH GREEN TOMATOES

2 tablespoons peanut, corn, or safflower oil
1 large onion, sliced
2 or 3 cloves garlic, sliced
3 pounds boneless beef rump roast, cut into 1-inch cubes
2 chorizo sausages, casings removed, crumbled
1 can (10 ounces) Mexican green tomatoes, with liquid
2 or 3 canned *chiles serranos*, drained, seeded, and chopped
3 tablespoons chopped coriander leaves
1 tablespoon capers
¼ teaspoon ground allspice
Salt and freshly ground pepper to taste
3 boiling potatoes (about 1 pound), pared, cubed, and cooked

1. In a large sauté pan, heat the oil and sauté the onion and garlic until golden; add the pieces of meat and brown. Remove the meat and set aside.

2. Add the chorizos to the pan and sauté until cooked through. Add the rest of the ingredients (except the potatoes); season with salt and pepper. Return the meat to the pan and simmer about 1½ hours, or until the meat is tender. Add the potatoes; heat through and serve.

Serves 6

FIAMBRE
COLD STEAK SALAD

The steak in this recipe must marinate several hours or overnight.

THE STEAK:
  2 pounds flank steak
  ¼ cup Dijon mustard
  2 cloves garlic, crushed
  2 tablespoons lemon or lime juice
  1 tablespoon Maggi seasoning
  ½ cup light Italian olive oil, vegetable oil, or corn oil
  1 teaspoon dried oregano

THE VEGETABLES:
  1 large, sweet red onion, sliced and separated into rings
  3 fresh *chiles poblanos* (California, Anaheim, or Güero), seeded and cut
    into thin strips
  1 canned *chile chipotle en vinagre*, drained, seeded, and chopped
  1 red bell pepper, seeded and deveined, cut into thin strips
  ½ pound green beans, cooked
  1 small ripe avocado, peeled and cut into small cubes
  1 pound boiling potatoes (about 3 medium), pared, cooked, and cooled

THE DRESSING:
  ½ cup light Italian olive oil
  1 large clove garlic, minced
  ¼ cup mild white vinegar
  1 tablespoon lemon or lime juice
  2 tablespoons Dijon mustard
  2 tablespoons chopped coriander leaves
  Salt and freshly ground pepper to taste

  1. Score the flank steak on both sides in a diamond pattern (to keep it from
curling as it broils).
  2. Combine the mustard, garlic, vinegar, lemon or lime juice, and Maggi
in a small bowl; whisk in the oil gradually until the marinade is creamy.
Brush the marinade over both sides of the steak and place the steak on a
platter. Marinate for several hours at room temperature or overnight in the
refrigerator (bringing to room temperature before broiling).
  3. Preheat the broiler to high.
  4. Remove the steak from marinade (reserve marinade) and broil in a
broiling pan on a rack set about 3 inches from heat. Broil about 5 minutes
on each side (this will produce a rare steak; cook longer to taste). Baste with
reserved marinade when turning. (The steak may, of course, be barbecued.)

5. Bring the steak to room temperature and slice diagonally against the grain into thin slices; cut each slice in half crosswise.

6. Place steak slices in a salad bowl with the vegetables. Place the dressing ingredients in a blender or in the workbowl of a food processor fitted with the steel blade and blend for 1 minute. Pour the dressing over the steak and vegetables; toss well and allow to marinate at room temperature for 1 hour before serving. (Makes 1 cup.)

VARIATION: If you have a cup or more of leftover rice, substitute it for the potatoes.

NOTE: The dressing for this dish is also delicious on a green salad or mixed salad of blanched vegetables.

Serves 6

AVES: POULTRY

Turkey is the only edible animal contributed by Mexico to world cookery. Other game birds were native to the country—pheasant, quail, and duckling among them—but turkey was the one that appealed to the Spanish eye and tongue. When the conquistadores discovered turkey, they were quick to introduce it to an enthralled Europe.

Because there were no domesticated animals other than dogs used in the Indian kitchen, game birds offered the only protein of significance—aside from beans—in the Mexican diet. Poultry recipes are thus some of the most ancient in the cuisine (haunch of enemy or shoulder of sacrificed warrior excepted). The birds were cooked, then the flesh shredded and served with a sauce of seeds and nuts—as poultry is often served in Mexico today.

In Mexico, turkeys and chickens are seldom roasted in the oven as they are in North America; they are usually sautéed or boiled. The most elaborate, complex, and unique of poultry dishes are the traditional *moles*, often made for feast days and other celebrations, which are discussed in the next chapter.

POLLO EN SALSA DE NUEZ
CHICKEN IN WALNUT SAUCE

5 tablespoons peanut, corn, or safflower oil
6 cloves garlic, chopped
3 whole chicken breasts, skinned, boned, and halved
3 dried *chiles anchos*, prepared as directed on page 16
1 large onion, finely chopped
1 cup walnuts, whole or broken into pieces
2 tablespoons chopped coriander leaves
½ teaspoon ground cinnamon
½ teaspoon ground cloves
¼ teaspoon ground allspice
Salt and freshly ground pepper to taste
1 cup chicken stock (homemade or canned)

THE CHICKEN:
1. Heat 3 tablespoons of the oil in a large skillet or sauté pan and sauté one-third of the garlic until just golden. Add the chicken breasts and sauté 5 minutes on each side. When the chicken is done, remove and set aside. Keep warm in a very low oven.

THE SAUCE:
2. Add the remaining 2 tablespoons oil to the skillet and sauté the onions

and remaining garlic until onion is translucent and limp.

3. Transfer onions and garlic to the workbowl of a food processor fitted with the steel blade and add the rest of the ingredients (except the chicken); process to a smooth purée.

4. Return the purée to the skillet and bring to a simmer. Cook for 5 minutes, stirring constantly. (The sauce should be the consistency of heavy cream. If it is too thick, add more chicken stock or a little water. If it is too thin, cook a few minutes longer to reduce.) Place the sautéed breasts in the sauce; cover and simmer 3 minutes more, until the breasts are heated through.

Serves 6

POLLO VERDE
GREEN CHICKEN

1 cup chopped coriander leaves
1 large onion, chopped
3 cloves garlic, chopped
4 romaine lettuce leaves, shredded
1 can (10 ounces) Mexican green tomatoes, with liquid
1 canned *chile jalapeño*, drained, seeded, and quartered
4 scallions, with greens, cut into 1-inch lengths
Salt and freshly ground pepper to taste
3 whole chicken breasts, skinned, boned, halved, and cut into ¾-inch
    slices
1 cup sour cream or yogurt

1. Combine coriander, onion, garlic, lettuce, green tomatoes (including liquid), chili, scallions, salt, and pepper in the workbowl of a food processor fitted with the steel blade. Process to a coarse purée. Taste for seasoning.

2. Pour the purée into a large sauté pan; bring to a simmer and cook, covered, for 30 minutes. Add the chicken pieces and continue to cook for 20 minutes more.

3. Remove chicken and sauce from heat and mix the sour cream. Return to low heat just to heat through. Transfer to a warm serving platter.

VARIATION: Pass a small bowl of grated Parmesan or shredded Monterey Jack cheese as a garnish.
Serve with fresh egg noodles dressed with butter and tossed with 2 tablespoons of toasted sesame seeds.

Serves 6

POLLO EN SALSA DE AJONJOLI
CHICKEN IN SESAME SAUCE

THE CHICKEN:
  Salt and freshly ground pepper to taste
  3 whole chicken breasts, skinned, boned, and cut into ½-inch strips
  ¼ cup lime juice
  2 cloves garlic, crushed

THE SAUCE:
  3 tablespoons (or more) peanut, corn, or safflower oil
  1 onion, finely chopped
  2 cloves garlic, minced
  ½ teaspoon ground cinnamon
  ½ teaspoon ground cloves
  ½ teaspoon freshly ground pepper
  1 cup sesame seeds, toasted
  1 can (16 ounces) Italian plum tomatoes, drained
  2 canned *chiles chipotles en vinagre*, drained
  1 cup chicken stock (homemade or canned)
  1 cup sour cream or *crème fraîche*

1. Salt and pepper the chicken pieces in a bowl and pour in the lime juice. Toss well and allow to marinate while making the sauce.

2. Heat 3 tablespoons oil in a sauté pan and sauté the onion and garlic along with the cinnamon, cloves, and pepper until the onion is wilted. Remove the onion mixture to the workbowl of a food processor fitted with the steel blade, leaving as much oil as possible in the pan. Add the sesame seeds, tomatoes, and chilies to the onion mixture and process to a smooth purée.

3. Add a little more oil to the pan if there isn't enough and sauté the chicken pieces, stirring, to brown lightly, on all sides (about 5 minutes). Remove with a slotted spoon and set aside. Pour the purée into the pan and cook over medium heat, scraping and stirring, for 3 or 4 minutes.

4. Lower the heat and simmer the sauce, uncovered, for 20 minutes more, scraping and stirring occasionally. Add the cup of stock and simmer 10 minutes more. Add the sautéed chicken and heat through for 5 minutes. Just before serving, stir in the sour cream over low heat. Mix thoroughly and transfer to a heated platter.

SUGGESTION: Serve with parsleyed new potatoes or baked potatoes to help absorb the sauce.

Serves 6

POLLO PIBIL
OVEN-BARBECUED CHICKEN IN THE STYLE OF YUCATÁN

The chicken in this recipe must marinate 24 hours.

½ cup orange juice
¼ cup lemon juice
Zest of 1 orange
Zest of 1 lemon
1 teaspoon freshly ground pepper
1 teaspoon salt
6 cloves garlic, quartered
1 tablespoon achiote (annatto) seeds
½ teaspoon dried oregano
½ teaspoon ground cumin
½ teaspoon ground allspice
1 large onion, finely chopped
1 chicken (4 pounds), cut in serving pieces

1. Place all the ingredients (except the chicken and onion) in the work-bowl of a food processor fitted with the steel blade and process to a smooth purée.

2. Coat each piece of chicken evenly with the purée; sprinkle with chopped onion and wrap each piece separately and tightly in aluminum foil. Place the wrapped bundles of chicken on a dish; allow to marinate for at least 24 hours in the refrigerator. Turn several times during the marinating period.

3. Preheat the oven to 350°F.

4. Set the foil-wrapped chicken pieces on a rack in a covered roasting pan. Pour water into the pan to a depth of 1 or 2 inches; cover and bake for 2½ hours. Serve each of your guests a wrapped chicken piece, and let them slit the packages open so they can enjoy the aroma. To be authentic, serve with hot tortillas.

Serves 6

POLLO EN SALSA DE NARANJA
CHICKEN IN ORANGE–SESAME SAUCE

THE CHICKEN:
1 roasting chicken (4 pounds)
Salt and freshly ground pepper to taste
½ teaspoon ground cinnamon
½ teaspoon ground turmeric
1 teaspoon ground coriander
¼ teaspoon ground cloves

THE SAUCE:
2 tablespoons peanut, corn, or safflower oil
2 medium onions, chopped

4 cloves garlic, minced
¾ cup orange juice
¼ cup water
¼ cup raisins
1 cup sesame seeds, toasted
2 tablespoons capers

THE GLAZE:
2 tablespoons cornstarch
¼ cup water
Zest of 1 orange, julienned (carve off zest with swivel-head potato peeler)
¼ cup orange marmalade

1. Rinse the chicken; drain and pat with paper toweling to dry. Sprinkle inside and out with salt and pepper. Combine the spices and rub over the outside of the chicken. Set aside.

2. In a 6-quart Dutch oven or a heavy kettle large enough to hold the chicken, heat the oil and sauté the onions and garlic, stirring until golden but not browned. Add the orange juice, water, raisins, sesame seeds, and capers; stir. Place the chicken in the pot, breast side up. Bring the liquid to a boil; reduce the heat, cover, and simmer, basting occasionally, 1 hour 15 minutes, or until the chicken is tender. Then remove the chicken to a warm serving platter.

3. Skim fat from the liquid left in the pot. Stir the cornstarch into the ¼ cup water and pour into the simmering liquid. Stir in the orange zest and marmalade. Cook until thickened. Pour or spoon evenly over the chicken.

NOTE: Surround the chicken with shredded lettuce and diced red bell pepper. Sprinkle with additional toasted sesame seeds.

Serves 6–8

POLLO EN SALSA DE CHILES VERDES Y MOSTAZA
CHICKEN IN GREEN CHILIES AND MUSTARD SAUCE

THE CHICKEN:
1 chicken (3½ pounds), cut into at least 4 serving pieces
Salt and freshly ground pepper to taste
½ cup all-purpose flour
2 tablespoons butter
2 tablespoons peanut, corn, or safflower oil
½ cup Dijon mustard

THE SAUCE:
1 medium onion, coarsely chopped
¼ pound mushrooms, coarsely chopped
⅓ cup dry sherry
⅓ cup chicken stock (homemade or canned)
1 can (4 ounces) chopped green chilies, drained
1 cup heavy cream

THE GARNISH:
¼ cup *pepitas* (pumpkin seeds), shelled and toasted

1. Preheat the oven to 350°F.

2. Rinse the chicken pieces and pat dry with paper toweling. Sprinkle with salt and pepper and dredge in flour, coating all sides.

3. In a large skillet or sauté pan, heat the butter and oil together. Add the chicken, skin side down (as many pieces as the pan will hold comfortably), and brown over medium heat, 5 minutes on each side. As the pieces are browned, transfer them to a large baking dish, arranging all the pieces of chicken, skin side up, in one layer in the dish. Coat the skin thickly with the mustard. Set aside.

4. In the butter and oil that remains in the skillet, sauté the onion over medium heat for about 5 minutes, or until translucent. Add the mushrooms, stir, and cook for 1 minute longer. Pour in the sherry and chicken stock; raise the heat to high and scrape the skillet with a wooden spoon, loosening all the browned particles. Add the green chilies; stir to combine, then remove the pan from the heat. Stir in the heavy cream.

5. Return the pan to low heat and cook for 5 minutes, being careful the cream does not boil. Pour the sauce over the chicken pieces and bake for 30 minutes. Serve from the baking dish or arrange on a warm serving platter. Sprinkle with *pepitas*.

Serves 4

PIPIÁN VERDE DE AJONJOLI
GREEN CHICKEN FRICASSEE WITH SESAME SEEDS

THE CHICKEN:
    1 roasting chicken (4 pounds), cut into serving pieces
    2 teaspoons salt
    1 teaspoon freshly ground pepper
    1 teaspoon paprika
    4 tablespoons butter
    2 tablespoons peanut, corn, or safflower oil
    1 cup dry white wine
    2 cups chicken stock (homemade or canned)
    1 bay leaf
    ¼ teaspoon white pepper
    2 sprigs parsley
    2 carrots, scraped and cut crosswise in 3
    1 whole onion stuck with 2 cloves

THE SAUCE:
    1 cup sesame seeds
    1 large onion, chopped
    4 cloves garlic, chopped
    ¼ cup chopped coriander leaves
    2 cans (10 ounces each) Mexican green tomatoes, drained, liquid reserved
    6 canned *chiles serranos*, drained and rinsed well
    2 tablespoons peanut, corn, or safflower oil
    2 egg yolks
    1 cup heavy cream

1. Rinse the chicken pieces and dry well with paper toweling. Mix together the salt, pepper, and paprika and rub the mixture into the chicken pieces.

2. In a large, heavy Dutch oven or casserole, heat the butter and 2 tablespoons oil and, when sizzling, add chicken pieces to fit in one layer. Brown the chicken about 3 minutes on each side. Remove to a platter. Repeat until all the chicken is browned, then return all pieces to the pot.

3. Add the wine, stock, bay leaf, pepper, parsley, carrots, and clove-studded onion to the pot. Bring to a boil over high heat; lower the heat and simmer, covered, for 1 hour, or until the chicken is tender. Remove the chicken to a platter and set aside. Slice the carrots into thin rounds and reserve. Strain the stock and pour back into the pot.

4. Pulverize the sesame seeds in a blender or food processor until they are as fine as possible; set aside. Combine the chopped onion, garlic, coriander, drained tomatoes, and chilies in the workbowl of a food processor fitted with the steel blade; process with several pulses to a coarse purée.

5. Heat 2 tablespoons of oil in a skillet; add the purée and the pulverized sesame seeds and fry for 2 or 3 minutes, stirring to keep the sauce from sticking.

6. Bring stock to a boil.

7. In a small bowl, whisk together the egg yolks and heavy cream. Add to this mixture a ladleful of the hot stock, whisking briskly to prevent curdling. Pour all this liquid into the pot of chicken stock and reduce the heat to a simmer. Add the purée to the pot and stir. Add some of the reserved tomato liquid *only* if the sauce is too thick (it should be only as thick as heavy cream). Cook for 5 minutes. Return the chicken pieces and sliced carrots to the sauce and heat through.

NOTE: Serve on a bed of egg noodles or with Arroz a la Mexicana (page 67), Arroz Amarillo (page 67), Arroz de Oro (page 67), or Arroz Blanco (page 66).

Serves 6

POLLO EN PIPIAN
CHICKEN IN PUMPKIN SEED SAUCE

This is a very elegant, very rich special occasion dish combining a Spanish method of preparing chicken breasts with a Mexican sauce.

THE CHICKEN:
    4 whole chicken breasts, skinned, boned, and halved
    Salt and white pepper to taste
    3 cups fresh bread crumbs or pulverized crisp fried tortillas
    1 cup sour cream or *crème fraîche*
    4 tablespoons butter
    ¼ cup peanut, corn, or safflower oil

THE SAUCE:

1 cup *pepitas* (pumpkin seeds), shelled and toasted
5 *chiles anchos*, prepared as directed on page 16
1 large onion, coarsely chopped
3 cloves garlic, coarsely chopped
½ teaspoon dried *epazote*, crumbled
1 can (16 ounces) Italian plum tomatoes, drained and chopped
2 tablespoons peanut, corn, or safflower oil
Salt and freshly ground pepper to taste
½ teaspoon sugar
Chicken stock (homemade or canned)

1. Place the halved chicken breasts between two sheets of waxed paper and pound them flat with a metal pounder or the wide blade of a meat cleaver. Season the breasts on both sides with salt and pepper.

2. Have the bread crumbs ready on a sheet of waxed paper. One at a time, coat the breasts on both sides with the sour cream, then with the bread crumbs, pressing the crumbs with the fingers to assure they adhere well.

3. Place the coated chicken breasts on a large platter; cover with waxed paper and refrigerate for several hours.

4. Melt the butter and ¼ cup oil in a large skillet. When they are sizzling, add the breasts several at a time. Brown over medium heat, about 6 minutes on each side. Keep the browned breasts warm in a low oven until all are cooked.

5. Pulverize the *pepitas* in a food processor fitted with the steel blade. Remove and set aside.

6. Combine the chilies, onion, garlic, *epazote*, and tomatoes in the un-rinsed workbowl and process to a coarse purée.

7. Heat 2 tablespoons oil in a skillet and add the *pepitas* and purée; stir over medium heat for 5 minutes. Add salt, pepper, and sugar to taste. Mix in some chicken stock, a little at a time, adding only enough to bring the sauce to the consistency of heavy cream. Arrange the chicken breasts on a serving platter and pour some of the sauce over them. Pass the rest of the sauce.

NOTE: The Sauce may be prepared ahead of time and kept warm or refrigerated and reheated.

SUGGESTIONS AND VARIATIONS: The breasts may be served without the sauce, accompanied by lime wedges. If you do serve them alone, try adding 2 tablespoons ground pecans or walnuts and a pinch of nutmeg to the sour cream before coating the breasts.

Serve the breasts with Salsa Almendra Verde (page 37) or Salsa Almendra Roja (page 37) instead of the *pipián*.

Serve the *pipián* over poached chicken breasts, or sautéed strips of boned breasts.

Serves 6–8

PAVO EN FRIO
YUCATECAN COLD SPICED TURKEY

THE TURKEY:
1 small turkey (7 to 8 pounds)
Salt and freshly ground pepper to taste
¼ pound Canadian bacon, cut in ½-inch cubes
6 cloves garlic, minced
3 avocado leaves, toasted and crumbled
2 tart apples, pared, cored, and cubed
½ teaspoon ground cinnamon
½ teaspoon ground cloves
½ teaspoon grated nutmeg
½ teaspoon ground allspice
2 cups chicken stock (homemade or canned)

THE SAUCE:
½ cup dry white wine
½ cup mild white vinegar
2 oranges, peeled and sectioned, membranes removed
1 teaspoon lemon juice
2 medium onions, sliced
1 bay leaf
½ teaspoon dried thyme
Salt and white pepper to taste

THE GARNISH:
18 pimiento-stuffed or pitted green olives
2 tablespoons capers

THE ARRANGEMENT:
Plain cooked white rice at room temperature
Vinaigrette dressing

1. Rinse the turkey and dry it with paper toweling inside and out. Sprinkle the cavity with salt and pepper and stuff with bacon, garlic, crumbled avocado leaves, and apples. Combine the spices and rub them over the outside of the bird. Wrap the turkey in cheesecloth, securing the ends with string.

2. Bring the stock to a boil in a large kettle; lower the turkey into the pot and cover tightly. Lower the heat and simmer for 1½ hours, or until tender. Remove the turkey from the pot and unwrap; then return to the pot.

3. Add the wine, vinegar, orange sections, lemon juice, onions, bay leaf, thyme, salt, and pepper to the pot. Cover and simmer for about 10 minutes, or until the onions are tender. Turn off the heat; remove the cover and allow the turkey to cool in the sauce until it is at room temperature.

4. Remove the turkey from the pot and cut into at least 10 serving pieces. Place the pieces on a serving platter and garnish with olives and capers. Moisten the turkey with a little of the sauce; transfer the rest of the sauce to a bowl and serve with the turkey.

5. Mix rice with vinaigrette dressing, and serve turkey at room temperature.

Serves 8–10

POLLO EN RELLENO DE PAN Y PACANAS
CHICKEN BREASTS WITH BREAD CRUMBS AND PECANS

THE CHICKEN:
    2 tablespoons peanut, corn, or safflower oil
    3 cloves garlic, chopped
    2 chorizo sausages, casings removed, sliced
    3 whole chicken breasts, skinned, boned, and halved

THE VEGETABLES:
    2 medium boiling potatoes, pared and cut into ½-inch cubes
    2 medium onions, coarsely chopped
    2 carrots, scraped, halved lengthwise, and sliced ¼-inch thick
    3 cloves garlic, quartered
    Salt and freshly ground pepper to taste

THE SAUCE:
    1 can (10 ounces) Mexican green tomatoes, with liquid
    ¼ cup raisins, plumped in a little dry sherry
    2 canned *chiles jalapeños en escabeche*, drained and chopped

THE TOPPING:
    1 tablespoon peanut, corn, or safflower oil
    1 tablespoon butter
    1 cup fresh bread crumbs
    ½ cup pecans broken in small pieces

1. Heat 2 tablespoons of oil in a skillet or sauté pan and cook the garlic over moderate heat until slightly golden. Add the chorizos and stir until cooked through and the fat has been rendered out. Add the chicken breasts and sauté, stirring, until just cooked. Remove the chicken pieces from the skillet and set aside.

2. Place the potatoes, onions, carrots, garlic, salt, and pepper in a saucepan with water to cover. Bring to a boil; reduce the heat and simmer, covered, for 15 to 20 minutes, until the vegetables are just tender. Do not overcook. Drain, reserving the stock. Set aside.

3. Purée the green tomatoes, with their liquid, in a food processor or blender.

4. Reheat the skillet containing the oil and chorizos and pour in the purée. Stir until heated, then add the raisins (with any unabsorbed sherry), 2 tablespoons of the reserved vegetable stock, and the chilies; simmer 10 minutes. Add the potatoes, carrots, onions, and garlic and stir to heat through. Add the chicken pieces and heat through.

5. Heat 1 tablespoon each of oil and butter in a small skillet. When sizzling, add the bread crumbs, stirring, until they are golden brown. Add the pecans and stir 2 or 3 minutes more, taking care not to burn them.

6. Turn the chicken mixture onto a warm platter; sprinkle with the bread crumb–pecan mixture and serve immediately.

SUGGESTION: Serve with hot tortillas and follow with a mixed green salad.

Serves 6–8

POLLO SOBRE PAPA MACHUCADA A LA GORDA
CHICKEN BREASTS ON A POUNDED POTATO

3 whole chicken breasts, skinned, boned, and cut into 1-inch strips
Salt and freshly ground pepper to taste
4 tablespoons butter
¼ cup peanut, corn, or safflower oil
1 large onion, thinly sliced
21 canned peeled green chilies, drained, 12 cut in strips, 9 left whole
½ cup milk
2 cups sour cream or *crème fraîche*
¼ pound Monterey Jack cheese, shredded
6 large baking potatoes, pared

1. Season the chicken breasts with salt and pepper.
2. Heat the butter and oil together in a sauté pan and sauté the chicken breasts for a few minutes on both sides until they are lightly browned. Remove and set aside.
3. In the fat left over from sautéing the chicken, sauté the onion until translucent and limp. Add the chili strips; cover and cook over medium heat for 5 minutes.
4. Blend the whole chilies, milk, and salt to taste in the workbowl of a food processor fitted with the steel blade until smooth. Add the sour cream and blend thoroughly.
5. Preheat the oven to 350°F.
6. Arrange the chicken in an ovenproof serving dish large enough to hold the chicken pieces in one layer. Cover with the onion-chili mixture and the sauce. Sprinkle evenly with cheese and bake for 30 minutes.
7. While the chicken is baking, place the potatoes and salt in a large kettle and cover with water. Bring to a boil and cook for 25 to 30 minutes to taste, or until fork tender.
8. Place a cooked potato on each of 6 dinner plates; crush the potatoes by pressing them with the bottom of a tumbler (or break up with a fork). Top each potato with chicken and sauce.

Serves 6

POLLO CON JUGO DE LIMA Y PACANAS
PECAN LIME CHICKEN

3 whole chicken breasts, skinned, boned, and halved
1 tablespoon coarse (kosher) salt
Freshly ground pepper
¼ cup lime juice
3 tablespoons butter
2 thick slices stale French bread
1 cup pecan meats
1 pound fresh, very ripe tomatoes or 1 can (16 ounces) Italian plum
    tomatoes, drained, liquid reserved

½ teaspoon freshly ground pepper
¼ teaspoon ground cloves
2 bay leaves, crumbled
¼ cup chicken stock (homemade or canned)

1. Season the chicken breasts with the salt and grind a generous amount of pepper over each. Pour the lime juice over them and allow them to marinate for at least 30 minutes.

2. Preheat the oven to 350°F.

3. Sauté the bread, torn in several pieces, in 1 tablespoon of the butter until a deep golden color. Transfer to the workbowl of a food processor fitted with the steel blade or a blender.

4. Add another tablespoon of butter to the pan and sauté the pecans for 1 minute.

5. Add the sautéed pecans, tomatoes, pepper, cloves, bay leaves, and chicken stock to the bread in the food processor or blender. Process to a fairly smooth paste (add some of the juice from the drained tomatoes, if paste is too thick).

6. Melt the remaining 1 tablespoon butter in the same pan used for the bread and pecans; pour into a shallow ovenproof casserole large enough to hold the chicken breasts in one layer. Spread about one-third of the pecan sauce evenly over the bottom of the pan and arrange the chicken breasts over it. Spread the remaining pecan sauce over the chicken and bake for 30 minutes, or until the chicken is cooked through and a light crust has formed on top.

SUGGESTION: Pass Salsa Verde (page 33) or thin strips of canned pickled *chiles jalapeños* on the side.

VARIATION: You may substitute almonds, cashews, or any nuts you prefer in this dish. Some nuts, however, are harder to process than others. You may need a little more liquid with almonds or hazelnuts, for instance.

Serves 6

MOLES AND TINGAS

Moles (rhymes with *olés*) are really Mexican stews. The method for preparing them, however, is different from that used in French or other European stew-cooking. It is similar, in fact, to methods used in India—although they were developed separately. In making *moles*, the usual Mexican seasoning ingredients—chilies, nuts, tomatoes, herbs, and spices—are ground to a paste or puréed in a blender or food processor, then fried in hot oil for several minutes while being stirred (to avoid burning). The meat is cooked separately in liquid. The seasoning mixture is then added to the meat, and the two are simmered together until the meat absorbs the flavor of the seasonings.

If the *mole* mixture is not fried first, the resulting dish will have a raw taste and the flavors will not blend properly. Because of the liquid in the tomatoes, the *mole* seasoning mixture can splatter when put into hot fat, so begin to stir *immediately* and then turn down the heat to simmer. It is also helpful to add some of the cooking liquid from the meat to the fried mixture to thin it out before transferring the seasoning mixture to the meat.

Tingas are indigenous to the city of Puebla, and are more European in method than *moles*. After the conquest, cooks in this area of Mexico adapted the Spanish technique of sautéing onions and garlic in fat (usually rendered from crumbled chorizo sausages), adding tomatoes, precooked meat, herbs, spices, *chiles chipotles*, and stock or other liquid; the whole mixture was then simmered for 10 or 15 minutes to allow the flavors to mingle. *Tingas* are a lovely way to use up leftover meats or chicken. By adding a little extra liquid or more tomatoes, you can make a *tinga* into a hearty spaghetti sauce.

MOLE VERDE DE CACAHUATE
PORK WITH PEANUTS IN GREEN SAUCE

THE PORK:
  3 pounds lean pork loin, cut into bite-size cubes
  1 medium onion, coarsely chopped
  4 cloves garlic, coarsely chopped
  1 tablespoon salt

THE SAUCE:
  6 ounces dry-roasted peanuts
  1 can (16 ounces) Mexican green tomatoes, drained
  ½ cup loosely packed coriander leaves, chopped
  ½ teaspoon freshly ground pepper
  2 tablespoons mild white vinegar
  3 fresh *chiles jalapeños*, seeded
  5 cloves garlic, quartered

2½ cups broth reserved from pork
2 tablespoons peanut, corn, or safflower oil
1 onion, thinly sliced
Salt

1. Place the pork, onion, and garlic in a saucepan and cover with water; add 1 tablespoon salt. Bring to a boil, then reduce to a simmer. Cook for 30 minutes or until tender. Remove the pork with a slotted spoon, reserving the broth.

2. While the pork is stewing, put the peanuts, green tomatoes, coriander, pepper, chilies, and garlic in the workbowl of a food processor fitted with the steel blade. Purée until smooth, adding a little pork broth if necessary.

3. Heat the oil in a sauté pan and sauté the onion until slightly wilted; add the pork and sauté until the onion is golden brown, stirring all the while to turn the pork pieces. Add the purée and cook for a few minutes, stirring and scraping so the sauce doesn't stick. Add 2 cups of broth, a little at a time, stirring. Taste for seasoning. Simmer for 15 minutes. (The sauce should be the consistency of heavy cream. If the sauce is too thick, add the remaining ½ cup of broth.)

NOTE: Traditionally, this dish is served with corn tortillas, but it is delicious with wheat tortillas fried in hot oil until they brown slightly and puff up.

Serves 6

MOLE DE PUERCO Y POLLO
PORK AND CHICKEN MOLE

THE MEATS:
   2 tablespoons peanut, corn, or safflower oil
   2 chorizo sausages, casings removed, chopped
   2 sweet Italian sausages, casings removed, chopped
   ½ pound boneless pork loin, cubed
   1 chicken (3 to 4 pounds), cut into serving pieces

THE SAUCE:
   6 *chiles anchos*, prepared as directed on page 16
   2 medium onions, coarsely chopped
   4 cloves garlic, quartered
   ½ can (28-ounce size) Italian plum tomatoes, drained and chopped
   2 tablespoons sesame seeds, toasted
   2 tablespoons *pepitas* (pumpkin seeds)
   ¼ cup almonds
   ¼ cup pecans, walnuts, or peanuts
   1 tablespoon mild white vinegar
   1 teaspoon dried oregano
   Salt and freshly ground pepper to taste
   2 cups chicken stock (homemade or canned)

1. Heat the oil in a large sauté pan and fry the sausage meat. Remove from the pan with a slotted spoon and set aside. In the oil remaining in the pan, fry the pork till browned. Remove with the slotted spoon and add to the sausage. Then sauté the chicken pieces until golden on both sides. Remove with the slotted spoon and set aside with the sausage and pork. Remove the fat from the pan.

2. In the workbowl of a food processor fitted with the steel blade, purée the chilies, onions, garlic, tomatoes, sesame seeds, *pepitas*, almonds, other nuts, vinegar, and oregano till smooth.

3. Pour the vegetable purée into the fat remaining in the pan and simmer for 5 minutes. Season the mixture with salt and pepper, then add the meats and chicken to the sauce, including any juices and drippings that may have accumulated. Mix well. Cover and simmer for 30 minutes. Pierce the chicken with a fork to determine if it is tender and done. Cook longer if necessary.

Serves 6

MOLE ROJO
RED PORK AND CHICKEN STEW WITH CHILES SERRANOS

THE PORK:
1 pound boneless lean pork for stew, cut into 1½-inch cubes
2 cloves garlic, halved
1 whole onion stuck with 2 cloves
2 sprigs parsley
1 tablespoon salt

THE MOLE:
1 can (16 ounces) Italian plum tomatoes, chopped, with liquid
2 cloves garlic, quartered
6 canned *chiles serranos*, drained and seeded
½ teaspoon dried oregano
½ teaspoon dried thyme
½ teaspoon dried *epazote*, crumbled
Salt and freshly ground pepper to taste
1 tablespoon peanut, corn, or safflower oil
Stock reserved from pork

THE CHICKEN:
1 chicken (3½ to 4 pounds) cut into serving pieces
2 teaspoons ground coriander

1. Place the pork, garlic, onion, and parsley in a saucepan and cover with water; add 1 tablespoon salt. Bring to a boil, then reduce to a simmer. Cook for 1 hour. Discard the vegetables; drain the pork, reserving stock, and set meat aside.

2. In the workbowl of a food processor fitted with the steel blade, combine the tomatoes with their liquid, garlic, chilies, oregano, thyme, *epazote*, salt, and pepper and process to a smooth purée.

3. Heat the oil in a large sauté pan add the purée. Cook, stirring constantly, over medium heat for 5 minutes; add the reserved pork stock. Cook, stirring, until heated through, then taste for seasoning.

4. Rub the chicken pieces with the ground coriander and add them to the sauce. Add the pork pieces, spooning sauce over all. Cover and simmer for 1 hour, or until the chicken is tender.

Serves 6

MOLE POBLANO DE GUAJOLOTE
TURKEY MOLE PUEBLAN STYLE

12 tablespoons peanut, corn, or safflower oil
1 turkey (8 pounds), cut into at least 10 serving pieces
3 *chiles chipotles*, seeded and deveined
1 pound fresh, ripe tomatoes, broiled whole (skins should be charred)
1 can (10 ounces) Mexican green tomatoes, drained
12 cups chicken stock (homemade or canned)
Salt
8 *chiles anchos*
4 *chiles mulatos*
4 *chiles pasillas*
1 teaspoon anise seeds
¾ cup sesame seeds
1 tortilla
1 slice white bread or 3 rounds of French bread
½ cup slivered blanched almonds
½ cup unsalted peanuts
½ cup raisins
2 large onions, chopped
6 cloves garlic, chopped
2 sprigs fresh coriander
½ teaspoon ground cloves
½ teaspoon ground coriander
1 teaspoon freshly ground pepper
1 teaspoon ground cinnamon
2 ounces Mexican chocolate or 2 squares (1 ounce each) unsweetened chocolate

1. In a large, heavy skillet, sauté pan, or Dutch oven heat 6 tablespoons of the oil and brown the turkey pieces well on all sides. Drain off excess oil, leaving the turkey pieces in the skillet.

2. Boil the *chiles chipotles* in water for 5 minutes. Drain and purée in the workbowl of a food processor fitted with the steel blade, along with the broiled tomatoes (with skins) and the green tomatoes. Add this purée to the turkey pieces and simmer, uncovered, until the liquid has evaporated. Add 4 cups of the chicken stock and 1 teaspoon salt; stir well, cover, and simmer for about 1 hour, or until the turkey is tender.

3. While chicken is simmering, prepare the *chiles anchos, mulatos,* and *pasillas* as directed on page 16.

4. In another skillet, heat 3 tablespoons of the remaining oil and fry the prepared chilies. Drain on paper toweling and purée in the processor. Reserve the oil in the skillet.

5. In a dry (ungreased) frying pan, toast the anise seeds and the sesame seeds separately, stirring constantly. Set aside.

6. Heat the remaining 3 tablespoons of oil in the same skillet used to fry the chilies. Fry each of the following ingredients separately, draining each on paper toweling: the tortilla, the bread, the almonds, the peanuts, and the raisins.

7. Break the tortilla and bread into pieces and add all the fried ingredients to the workbowl of the processor. Add the fried chilies, ½ cup of the sesame seeds (reserving ¼ cup for garnish), the anise seeds, onions, garlic, and fresh coriander. Purée, adding just enough chicken broth to make a smooth purée. Pour this into the pan containing the turkey.

8. To the turkey and purée, add the cloves, ground coriander, pepper, and cinnamon and stir over moderate heat. Add the chocolate and cook until melted. Continue cooking for 10 minutes more, stirring so that the sauce doesn't stick. Add the remaining chicken broth; heat through. Add more salt, if necessary, and simmer for about 20 minutes. Serve sprinkled with the remaining sesame seeds.

SUGGESTION: Serve with unfilled tamales or hot tortillas, Guacamole (page 38), Frijoles Refritos (page 120), and/or Arroz Blanco (page 66).

NOTE: The sauce can be as thick as sour cream or just thick enough to coat the back of a spoon. You decide. If it is too thick for your taste, add more broth. If it is too thin, add less broth at the end or cook the sauce down. Leftover *mole* sauce freezes well and can be used to delicious advantage in many tortillas and enchilada dishes. Experiment.

VARIATIONS: Substitute two 4-pound chickens if turkey does not appeal to you.

Substitute a 5-pound pork loin, bone in, for the turkey, braising the loin well before proceeding with the recipe.

Serves up to 10

TINGA POBLANO
PUEBLAN PORK STEW

THE PORK:
  2 tablespoons peanut, corn, or safflower oil
  3 pounds boneless pork shoulder, cut into 1½-inch cubes
  1 teaspoon salt

THE SAUCE:
  2 or 3 chorizo sausages, cases removed, crumbled or sliced thin
  2 onions, chopped
  3 cloves garlic, sliced
  1 can (16 ounces) Italian plum tomatoes, partially drained
  ½ teaspoon dried oregano
  ¼ teaspoon dried thyme
  1 bay leaf
  ½ teaspoon sugar

106

2 canned *chiles chipotles en vinagre,* chopped
1 tablespoon liquid from can of *chipotles*
Salt and freshly ground pepper to taste
½ cup stock reserved from pork
12 or more tiny new potatoes, boiled in their skins

THE GARNISH:
1 ripe avocado, peeled and thinly sliced
1 cup shredded romaine lettuce

1. Heat the oil in a large sauté pan and brown the pork well. Drain off the oil from the pan; add water just to cover the pork then add the salt. Cook, covered, over medium heat for about 30 minutes, or until the pork is tender. Drain off the stock and reserve. Set the pork aside.

2. Place the chorizos in the sauté pan and sauté, stirring to crumble further, until the fat has been rendered out. Add the onions and garlic to the sausages and sauté, stirring, until the onion is translucent and wilted. Add the rest of the ingredients for the sauce (except the stock and potatoes). Cook over high heat, stirring, for about 5 minutes. Stir in ½ cup of the reserved broth and the pork. Adjust the seasoning and simmer, uncovered, for about 10 minutes.

3. Add the boiled potatoes and simmer another 5 minutes. Remove the bay leaf. Garnish with sliced avocado and shredded lettuce.

SUGGESTION: Use as a topping for tostadas and garnish with the avocado and lettuce. Cook the sauce down if there is too much liquid. Ample for 12 tostadas.

Serves 6

MARISCOS Y PESCADOS: SHELLFISH AND FISH

Bordering the Pacific Ocean, the Gulf of Mexico, and the Caribbean, Mexico has thousands of miles of coastline, and so offers and consumes a great abundance of fish and shellfish. Varieties such as bluefish, mackerel, red snapper, cod, pompano, striped bass, flounder, tuna, shrimp, oysters, squid, octopus, crab, conch, clams, crayfish, and mussels are common to the waters and menus of both Mexico and the United States. Cooking methods are the same, too—poaching, baking, grilling, sautéing, frying. It is the combination of ingredients, the seasonings, that distinguish Mexican fish and shellfish dishes from all others. The use of nuts, *pepitas*, fruits, chilies, and citrus in the sauces is unique.

CAMARONES EN SALSA DE AJONJOLI
SHRIMP IN SESAME CREAM SAUCE

1 pound medium shrimp
1 tablespoon butter
Salt and freshly ground pepper to taste
1 clove garlic, thinly sliced
1 cup bottled clam juice
6 sprigs coriander
3 canned *chiles serranos*, drained and seeded
1 small onion, chunked
1 cup sesame seeds, toasted
1 cup sour cream or *crème fraîche*

1. Peel and devein the shrimp and sauté in a skillet or small sauté pan for 2 minutes in the butter with salt, pepper, and the garlic. Remove the shrimp and set aside.
2. Place the rest of the ingredients (except the sour cream) in the workbowl of a food processor fitted with the steel blade. Process until smooth. Add the purée to the skillet in which the shrimp were sautéed; bring to a boil, scraping and stirring, then lower the heat and simmer for about 10 minutes.
3. Stir the shrimp into the sauce and add the sour cream. Heat through but do not allow to boil. Serve immediately.

Serves 4

TIBURÓN EN SALSA DE NARANJA CON ARROZ VERDE
BABY MAKO SHARK IN ORANGE SAUCE ON GREEN RICE

2 pounds baby mako shark, cut into six steaks
All-purpose flour
Salt and white pepper to taste
3 tablespoons fresh parsley, chopped
4 cloves garlic, crushed
¼ cup light Italian olive oil
1 teaspoon lime juice
Juice of 4 medium oranges
Arroz Verde I or II (pages 68 or 69)

1. Preheat the oven to 450°F.
2. Dredge the fish steaks in flour seasoned with salt and pepper.
3. In a small bowl, mix together the parsley, garlic, olive oil, and lime juice. Spread this mixture over both sides of the fish steaks and place them in one layer in an ovenproof casserole. Pour the orange juice over the fish, cover, and bake for 20 minutes, or until the fish turns white and flakes easily with a fork. Serve over the rice.

NOTE: Baby shark (especially baby mako shark) is available at many good fish markets. They are *very* inexpensive and taste a lot like sword fish—only moister. Substitute sword fish, if you prefer.

Serves 6

MARISCOS EN MIGAS DE PAN DE MAIZ
SCALLOPS WITH CRUNCHY, CRUMBLED FRIED CORN BREAD

4 tablespoons butter
1 medium onion, chopped
3 cloves garlic, thinly sliced
½ teaspoon (or more) freshly ground pepper
Salt
2 *chiles jalapeños*, minced
1 cup crumbled corn bread
1½ pounds sea or bay scallops
2 tablespoons chopped parsley

1. Melt 2 tablespoons of the butter in a skillet. Sauté the onion and garlic until golden; add the chilies, the pepper, and salt to taste and sauté a few minutes more. Scrape the onion mixture into a bowl and set aside.
2. Melt the remaining 2 tablespoons butter in the skillet and, when foaming, toss in the crumbled corn bread. Sauté until crisp and deep golden brown. Scrape into the bowl with the onion mixture.

3. Add the scallops to the skillet and sauté in the butter remaining there until the scallops turn white, stirring all the while.

4. Stir onion mixture and corn bread crumbs into the scallops; heat through until the moisture is absorbed. Sprinkle with parsley, toss once more, and serve.

Serves 4

FILLETAS DE PESCADO BLÁNCO EN SALSA DE ALMENDRA
LEMON SOLE IN ALMOND AND CORIANDER SAUCE

2 cups court bouillon or bottled clam juice
3 pounds lemon sole fillets
3 tablespoons light Italian olive oil
3 cloves garlic, minced
1 slice French bread or half of a hard roll
½ cup blanched almonds, chopped
3 canned *chiles serranos*
1 generous handful of fresh coriander leaves
Salt and freshly ground pepper
¼ cup toasted shredded coconut

1. In a large skillet, add the fish fillets to boiling bouillon or clam juice; reduce to simmer and poach until the fish flakes easily with a fork—about 5 or 6 minutes. Remove fish from liquid, reserving liquid. Arrange fish carefully on a warm serving dish and keep warm in a very low oven.

2. Wipe out skillet with paper towel, add oil, and heat; add the garlic and brown the bread on both sides. Break or chop the bread coarsely.

3. Combine the bread and garlic, almonds, chilies, coriander, and poaching liquid in the container of a food processor fitted with the steel blade. Process until smooth. Pour into skillet and heat to barely bubbling. Add salt and pepper to taste and pour over the fillets. Sprinkle with toasted coconut and serve immediately.

Serves 6

PESCADO EN SALSA DE AJOS
RED SNAPPER IN GARLIC SAUCE

8 cloves garlic, finely minced
6 tablespoons light Italian olive oil
6 red snapper fillets (3 to 4 pounds)
Juice of 3 oranges
Salt and freshly ground pepper to taste
3 tablespoons chopped parsley

1. Combine half the garlic with half the oil and brush on both sides of the fillets. Marinate the fillets in a shallow baking dish for at least 1 hour.

2. Preheat the oven to 375°F.

3. Pour half the orange juice over the fillets; sprinkle with salt and pepper and place in the oven. Bake 15 or 20 minutes, or until the fish flakes easily when tested with a fork. While the fish is baking, follow step 4.

4. Heat the oil and sauté the remaining garlic in a small skillet, stirring, for 2 or 3 minutes, until it is just golden. Add the parsley, remaining orange juice, and salt and pepper to taste, simmer for 5 minutes.

5. Remove the fish from the oven; pour the sauce over the fish and serve. (Or carefully transfer the fillets to a warm serving platter; pour the sauce over and serve).

Serves 6

JAIBAS RELLENAS
STUFFED CRABS

2 tablespoons light Italian olive oil
2 cloves garlic, finely chopped
1 medium onion, finely chopped
½ green bell pepper, finely chopped
2 tablespoons Madeira wine or sweet sherry
2 canned Italian plum tomatoes, drained and chopped
1 tablespoon finely chopped parsley
2 canned *chiles serranos*, drained and finely chopped
1½ pounds fresh lump crab meat, picked over to remove bones or cartilage
Salt and freshly ground pepper to taste
¼ cup heavy cream, sour cream, or *crème fraîche*
2 cups fresh bread crumbs
2 tablespoons butter

1. Preheat the oven to 350°F.

2. Heat the oil in a skillet and add the garlic, onion, and green pepper. Sauté over medium heat for 1 minute, or until soft. Stir in the Madeira, tomatoes, parsley, and chilies and cook about 5 minutes until the mixture is almost dry.

3. Stir in the crab meat; turn the heat to high and cook until any liquid is absorbed. Season with salt and pepper.

4. Remove from the heat; add the cream and 1 cup of the bread crumbs. Mix well. Divide the mixture among 6 well-buttered ramekins or mound in scallop shells. Sprinkle each with a few spoonfuls of bread crumbs.

5. Melt the 2 tablespoons butter and drizzle over each ramekin. Bake on a cookie sheet in the center of the oven for 20 minutes, or until browned.

VARIATION: Sprinkle each ramekin or shell with grated Parmesan or Monterey Jack cheese before topping with bread crumbs and butter. Add 2 tablespoons of Dijon mustard along with the heavy cream.

Serves 6

PESCADO EN SALSA DE CILANTRO
FISH IN CORIANDER SAUCE

1 can (16 ounces) Italian plum tomatoes, partially drained (some liquid
   reserved) and coarsely chopped
1 medium onion, finely chopped
2 cloves garlic, finely chopped
2 cups chopped coriander leaves
1 canned *chile serrano* or *jalapeño*, seeded and chopped
¼ cup lime juice
Salt and freshly ground pepper
6 red snapper fillets or fillets of any firm, white-fleshed fish
½ cup pimiento-stuffed green olives or 2 tablespoons capers

1. Preheat the oven to 400°F.
2. Combine all the ingredients (except the fish and olives) in a large bowl.
3. Spread some of the mixture in a greased, baking dish just large enough
to hold the fillets in one layer. Place the fillets on top and cover with the
remaining sauce. Bake for 15 to 20 minutes, or until the fish flakes easily
when tested with a fork. Add a little of the drained tomato liquid or water
if the sauce seems dry. Garnish with olives or capers.

Serves 6

HUEVOS: EGGS

The Spanish introduced domesticated fowl and egg dishes to Mexican
cuisine. The Mexicans took them from there and created their own, more
hearty, alterations, combining eggs with tortillas, chilies, dried beef, cactus, ham, beans, seafood, sausage, potatoes, and more. They also gave many
of these dishes somewhat bizarre names—"eggs in rags and tatters," for one.

Mexican cooks have now invented new flavors for soufflés and quiche-
like preparations that are too intriguing to leave out, in spite of the fact that
they are basically un-Mexican in method and conception.

HUEVOS REVUELTOS Y CHORIZOS
CHORIZO HASH AND EGGS

6 chorizo sausages, casings removed, crumbled
3 medium onions, chopped
6 medium potatoes, pared, cut into ½-inch dice and boiled
6 eggs
2 tablespoons butter

1. Heat a large frying pan and cook the chorizos on medium heat until the fat has been rendered out. Add the onions and sauté until translucent and limp. Stir in the potatoes and press the mixture evenly over the bottom of the pan. Fry until a nice crust forms on the bottom.

2. Fry or scramble 6 eggs in butter. When done, portion out the hash on 6 plates and top with a fried egg or some scrambled eggs. Serve immediately.

VARIATION: If you have any leftover Picadillo (page 76), extend it with some fried chorizo and cooked potatoes. Serve under eggs.

Serves 6

HUEVOS EN SALSA DE JITOMATES
POACHED EGGS IN TOMATO SAUCE

3 tablespoons peanut, corn, or safflower oil
1 can (35 ounces) Italian plum tomatoes, drained (liquid reserved) and chopped
1 small onion, chopped
3 cloves garlic, finely chopped
2 cups water
1 teaspoon salt
½ teaspoon freshly ground pepper
¼ teaspoon ground coriander
½ canned *chile jalapeño*, seeded and chopped
1 dozen eggs
1 cup grated Monterey Jack or mild cheddar cheese

1. In a large sauté pan, heat the oil and cook the drained tomatoes, onion, and garlic, stirring and scraping, until they are reduced to a thick sauce. Add the water, reserved tomato liquid, salt, pepper, ground coriander, and chili, and bring to a boil; reduce the heat and simmer 10 minutes, covered. (If too much liquid has been lost in the cooking, add a little more water and simmer 5 minutes more.)

2. Break the eggs, one at a time, into a saucer or cup and carefully slide each egg from its saucer into the simmering broth. Sprinkle each with a little cheese; cover the pan and poach the eggs about 6 to 8 minutes until just set.

3. Remove the eggs from the sauce with a slotted spoon. Put 2 eggs in shallow soup bowls and spoon sauce over them.

SUGGESTION: Serve with hot tortillas or crusty French bread.

Serves 6

TORTILLA DE HUEVOS CAMPESINOS
PEASANT OMELET

3 tablespoons peanut, corn, or safflower oil
2 baking potatoes, less than ½ pound each, pared and very thinly sliced
Salt and freshly ground pepper to taste
½ teaspoon dried oregano
1 medium onion, halved and thinly sliced
1 cup cooked pork loin, from Cochinita Pibil (page 83) or any leftover
   pork, cut into ½-inch dice
1 dozen eggs
2 tablespoons finely chopped parsley
Pinch of cayenne pepper
2 tablespoons water
2 tablespoons butter

1. Heat the oil in a skillet. Add the potatoes and spread them out evenly without breaking the slices. Cook on one side for about 10 minutes, until they are nicely browned, lifting them gently with a spatula once in a while to be sure they don't stick. Sprinkle with salt, pepper, and oregano. Add the onion; again spread evenly. Cook for a minute or two more. Add the pork. Let cook while you prepare the eggs. Do not stir.

2. Beat the eggs with a fork or wire whisk. Add salt, pepper, parsley, and cayenne. Beat in the water and pour the eggs over the potato mixture. Allow to cook for a minute, then lift the mixture around the edges and add the 2 tablespoons butter underneath. As you lift, allow the uncooked egg to flow underneath. Shake the pan to be sure the egg is not sticking. While the egg is still loose on top, place a large plate or round serving platter over the skillet and, holding it in place, quickly invert the omelet onto the plate. Cut into pie-shaped wedges and serve immediately.

Serves 6

SOUFFLÉ CON CHILES VERDES
SOUFFLÉ WITH GREEN CHILIES

2 cups milk
6 large eggs
3 tablespoons plus 2 teaspoons butter
¼ cup flour
Salt and freshly ground pepper to taste
¼ teaspoon dried oregano
¼ teaspoon dried thyme
¼ teaspoon ground coriander
Pinch of cayenne pepper
2 teaspoons cornstarch
1 tablespoon water
¼ pound Gruyère or Monterey Jack cheese, grated
¼ cup grated Parmesan cheese
1 can (4 ounces) chopped green chilies, drained or ¼ cup *nopalitos,*
    canned in brine, drained and cut in tiny dice

1. Preheat the oven to 375°F.
2. In a saucepan, heat the milk to the boiling point but do not boil.
3. Separate the eggs and place the whites in a large mixing bowl or the bowl of an electric mixer.
4. Melt the 3 tablespoons butter in a saucepan and stir in the flour with a wire whisk. When smooth, add the hot milk, stirring rapidly with the whisk. Add salt, pepper, herbs, and spices and cook, stirring briskly, for 5 minutes. In a small bowl, blend the cornstarch and water and add it to the milk mixture, still stirring. Remove the pan from the heat and add the egg yolks. Continue to stir briskly. Blend in the cheeses and the chilies. Set the sauce aside.
5. Beat the egg whites until stiff. Add one-third of the whites to the sauce and fold in with the whisk. Add the sauce to the remaining whites and fold in gently with a rubber spatula until all is evenly blended.
6. Grease a 5-cup soufflé mold with the 2 teaspoons butter; add the Parmesan cheese and tilt and turn the dish until it is well coated with the cheese. Allow loose cheese to remain in the dish. Pour the egg mixture into the soufflé dish, scraping the mixing bowl with a spatula to get all of the soufflé into it, and bake in the oven for 35 to 40 minutes until the soufflé is puffed and browned. Serve immediately.

SUGGESTION: Serve with warm Salsa de Jitomate (page 34).

Serves 4

HUEVOS REVUELTOS CON SALSA
SCRAMBLED EGGS WITH SAUCE

THE SAUCE:
2 tablespoons peanut, corn, or safflower oil
3 canned peeled green chilies, drained and cut into strips
1 small onion, minced
1 large clove garlic, minced
1 can (16 ounces) Italian plum tomatoes, drained (some liquid reserved)
  and chopped
1 canned *chile serrano*, drained and finely chopped
Salt and freshly ground pepper to taste

THE EGGS:
8 eggs, beaten
¼ cup shredded Monterey Jack cheese

1. Heat the oil in a skillet and fry the green chilies, onion, and garlic.
When the onion is limp and turning golden, add the tomatoes, 2 tablespoons of the tomato liquid, and the *chile serrano*. Cook over medium heat,
stirring, until the sauce is reduced a little and thickened. Season with salt
and pepper.

2. Add the beaten eggs to the skillet and stir until the eggs are almost set;
fold in the cheese and lower the heat. Leave on the heat until cheese starts
to melt.

SUGGESTION: To be authentic, serve immediately with hot tortillas.

Serves 4

HUEVOS RANCHEROS
RANCH-STYLE EGGS

Sauce from Huevos Revueltos con Salsa (see above)
4 tablespoons peanut, corn, or safflower oil
8 eggs
4 tortillas
¼ pound Monterey Jack cheese, thinly sliced

1. Prepare the sauce; keep warm.

2. In a large, heavy skillet, heat 2 tablespoons of the oil; break the eggs into
the hot oil and cook until the whites are almost cooked through. Tip the pan
to baste the eggs with hot oil until the tops are slightly cooked. Remove to
a plate and keep warm.

3. Add the other 2 tablespoons of oil to the skillet; bring to the smoking
point and quickly cook each of the tortillas until soft. Drain on paper toweling. Place each tortilla on a warm serving plate; top with 2 fried eggs
(yolks unbroken). Spoon the warm sauce over the eggs and decorate with
cheese slices. Run under the broiler for a minute to melt the cheese. Serve
immediately.

VARIATION: Spread each tortilla with a generous layer of warm Frijoles Refritos (page 120), top with eggs, sauce, and cheese, and run under the broiler. Serve sprinkled with chopped coriander leaves.

Serves 4

CHORIZOS Y ESPINACA ENVUELTOS EN MASA HARINA
SAUSAGE AND SPINACH MASA ROLL

This soufflé can be used with any number of fillings.

THE SOUFFLÉ:
Melted butter and Quaker *masa harina* for greasing and flouring pan
4 tablespoons butter
½ cup Quaker *masa harina*
Salt and white pepper to taste
2 cups milk
5 eggs, separated
1 *chile jalapeño* (canned or fresh), seeded, deveined, and minced

1. Preheat the oven to 400°F.
2. Butter a 15½×10½×1-inch jelly-roll pan; line with waxed paper. Butter the paper well and dust lightly with *masa harina*.
3. Melt 4 tablespoons butter in a saucepan over low heat; whisk in ½ cup *masa harina*, salt, and pepper. Gradually whisk in the milk and bring to a boil. Remove the pan from the heat; stir in the minced chilies and set aside to cool.
4. Beat the egg yolks in a small bowl and add a little of the hot mixture, stirring. Pour the egg yolk mixture into the saucepan and cook over medium heat 1 minute longer, stirring. Do not allow to boil. Remove the pan from the heat; stir in the remaining chili-milk mixture and set aside to cool.
5. Beat the egg whites until stiff but not dry. Fold into the cooled sauce. Pour into the prepared jelly-roll pan and bake for 30 minutes, until puffed and browned. Turn out the soufflé immediately, upside-down, onto a fresh sheet of waxed paper. Carefully remove the waxed paper covering the soufflé. Spread with the warm filling and roll, starting with one of the long sides, lifting the fresh waxed paper to help roll it. Serve immediately or reheat later on an unbuttered cookie sheet for 15 to 20 minutes in a preheated 350°F oven.

Serves 6

SAUSAGE AND SPINACH FILLING:
2 tablespoons butter
½ pound chorizo sausages, casings removed, chopped
1 medium onion, coarsely chopped
¼ pound mushrooms, coarsely chopped

1 package (10 ounces) frozen chopped spinach, thawed and thoroughly
     drained or 1 pound fresh spinach, washed, drained, and coarsely
     chopped
6 ounces cream cheese, at room temperature
$\frac{1}{4}$ teaspoon grated nutmeg
Salt and freshly ground pepper to taste
$\frac{1}{4}$ cup freshly grated Monterey Jack or mild white cheddar cheese

1. Melt the butter in a skillet; add the chorizos and cook over medium heat
until the meat is browned, about 5 minutes. Add the onion and sauté 1
minute longer. Add the mushrooms and cook for another 2 or 3 minutes.
Mix in the spinach and heat through (if using fresh spinach, sauté until just
wilted).

2. Remove the pan from the heat and mash in the cream cheese with a
fork, adding nutmeg, salt, pepper, and Monterey Jack. Return to the heat
briefly to heat through. Stir, then spread the filling evenly over the soufflé.
Roll as directed.

VERDURAS: VEGETABLES

Many indigenous Mexican vegetables are, unfortunately, unavailable in United States markets. But because Mexicans rarely eat "plain" vegetables anyway, we can substitute those that are available here and cook them in Mexican sauces with Mexican techniques.

In Mexico, vegetables are often served as a separate course. Some vegetable dishes are elaborate and hearty enough to be the main course of a luncheon or supper menu; served in small portions, these are perfect with grilled, roasted, baked, or broiled meats, fish, or poultry. Other, less elaborate vegetable recipes have been adapted by Mexican cooks from the European repertoire and given that inevitable Mexican twist.

BEANS

Beans, an important part of Mexican cuisine, are available in the United States. Black, pinto, kidney, and pink California beans are all easy to come by anywhere in this country.

The main source of protein in the Aztec diet, beans were usually boiled, but when young and tender were often eaten fresh. Refried beans, popular everywhere in the country today, became a staple of the diet only after the Spanish introduced domesticated animals to the country (pre-Cortés Mexicans did not extract cooking oil from seeds and had no meat except for wild game from which to render fat). Beans are still a major source of protein in meat-poor areas and are as essential to the Mexican meal as potatoes or rice are to ours.

In the United States, beans usually come dried and are sold loose or packed in paper, cloth, boxes, or plastic bags. No matter how you buy dried beans, rinse and sort through them to remove any debris. Some bean varieties are also available canned; drain these before using.

FRIJOLES
BASIC BEANS

2 cups dried black, pinto, kidney, or pink beans
2 onions, finely chopped
4 cloves garlic, chopped
1 bay leaf or ½ teaspoon dried *epazote*
2 tablespoons peanut, corn, or safflower oil
1 tablespoon salt (or to taste)
Freshly ground pepper to taste

Put the beans in a saucepan and cover with cold water. Cover and bring to a boil. Add the onions, garlic, and bay leaf and lower the heat to a simmer. Cook gently for 1½ to 2 hours, adding more boiling water as it boils away. When the bean skins are soft, wrinkled, and breaking open, add the oil, salt, and a generous amount of freshly ground pepper. Continue simmering for another 30 minutes but add no more water. (There should be a good deal of liquid when the beans are done; the beans should be thoroughly soft, almost mushy.)

Serves 6

FRIJOLES REFRITOS
REFRIED BEANS

1 recipe Basic Beans (page 119)
6 tablespoons peanut, corn, or safflower oil
1 onion, finely chopped
2 cloves garlic, chopped
1 fresh, ripe tomato, peeled, seeded, and chopped

1. Purée the beans roughly in a food processor. (Do not purée beans in a blender, as they require too much liquid. If you do not have a food processor, it is best to mash the beans after you put them in the skillet, a few tablespoons at a time.)
2. Heat 2 tablespoons of the oil in a skillet; add the onion and garlic and sauté until the onion is translucent and limp. Add the tomato and cook 2 or 3 minutes. Add a little of the remaining oil and a few tablespoons of the puréed beans. Mash to incorporate the vegetables. Add more oil and beans, mashing and stirring with each addition, until all the beans are incorporated and you have a thick, creamy, somewhat dry paste.

Serves 6

ZUCCHINI Y ZANAHORIAS CON MENTA FRESCA
ZUCCHINI AND CARROTS WITH FRESH MINT

3 tablespoons butter
4 carrots, scraped and cut into ¼-inch slices
Salt and freshly ground pepper to taste
4 zucchini (each about 8 inches long), cut in half lengthwise then cut into
    ¼-inch slices
3 tablespoons chopped fresh mint leaves or fresh basil leaves

Heat the butter to sizzling in a skillet or sauté pan; add the carrots and plenty of salt and pepper. Cover and cook for 5 minutes over medium heat. Add the zucchini; cover and cook at the same temperature 5 minutes more. Serve sprinkled with the mint leaves.

Serves 6

ZANAHORIAS CRISTALIASADAS
GLAZED CARROTS

1½ pounds carrots, scraped and cut into ¼-inch slices
1 tablespoon granulated sugar
½ teaspoon salt
2 tablespoons butter
2 tablespoons (packed) brown sugar
¼ teaspoon ground ginger or 1 teaspoon finely chopped fresh ginger
¼ cup beef or chicken stock (homemade or canned)
Salt and freshly ground pepper to taste
¼ teaspoon allspice
1 tablespoon chopped parsley

1. Place the carrots in a saucepan with water to cover; add the granulated sugar and salt. Bring to a boil over high heat. Lower the heat to medium and simmer, covered, for about 10 minutes. Drain.
2. Heat the butter to sizzling in a skillet and add the carrots. Toss to coat. Sprinkle with the brown sugar and ginger and continue to toss until the carrots begin to glaze. Pour the stock over the carrots and cook, uncovered, until the liquid has cooked down. Season with salt, pepper, and allspice and sprinkle with parsley before serving.

Serves 4–6

HABICHUELAS Y ZANAHORIAS CON CHORIZO
GREEN BEANS AND CARROTS WITH CHORIZO

1 tablespoon butter
1 chorizo sausage, casing removed, crumbled
3 carrots, scraped and cut into ¼-inch sticks, then 2-inch lengths
½ pound green beans, cut into 2-inch lengths
1 teaspoon lemon juice
1 tablespoon Dijon mustard
Salt and freshly ground pepper to taste

Melt the butter in a skillet and add the chorizo. Sauté until most of the fat has been rendered out. Add the carrots and cook, covered, for 5 minutes. Stir in the string beans and cook, covered, 5 minutes more or until vegetables are crisp tender. Turn the heat to low. Stir in the lemon juice, mustard, salt, and pepper.

Serves 4

LENTEJAS CON PIÑA, PLATANO, Y MANZANA
LENTILS WITH PINEAPPLE, BANANA, AND APPLE

½ cup dried lentils
2 tablespoons raisins
2 cloves garlic, chopped
1 small onion, chopped
1 large fresh, ripe tomato, peeled and chopped, or 3 canned Italian plum
  tomatoes, drained and chopped
1½ tablespoons peanut, corn, or safflower oil
1 thick slice fresh pineapple, cut into chunks, or ⅔ cup canned pineapple
  chunks, drained
½ medium-sized firm banana, peeled and sliced
1 small cooking apple, pared, cored, and diced
Salt and freshly ground pepper to taste

1. Rinse the lentils and place in a saucepan with the raisins and water to
cover. Bring to a boil; reduce the heat and simmer for 45 minutes. Drain and
set aside.

2. Place the garlic, onion, and tomato in the workbowl of a food processor fitted with the steel blade. Process to a smooth purée. Heat the oil in
a skillet over high heat and cook the purée, stirring and scraping the skillet, for 3 minutes. Lower the heat to a simmer and add the pineapple, banana, apple, salt, and pepper. Simmer for 5 minutes more.

3. Add lentils to the purée and fruit and simmer over low heat, uncovered, for 10 minutes, stirring every so often. The lentils should be fairly dry
and have a creamy texture.

Serves 6

CHILES RAJAS Y PAPAS A LA CREMA
POTATOES AND STRIPS OF CHILI WITH CREAM

2 tablespoons peanut, corn, or safflower oil
1 large onion, halved, and thinly sliced
4 canned *chiles poblanos* (California, Anaheim, or Güero) or 4 fresh
  poblanos prepared as directed on page 17 and cut into ½-inch strips
4 medium boiling potatoes, pared, cubed, and cooked
1 cup heavy cream
Salt and freshly ground pepper to taste

1. Heat the oil in a skillet and fry the onion, stirring, until golden. Add
the chili strips. The oil will take on a green tone from the chilies. When it
does, gently stir in the potatoes and cook a few minutes longer.

2. Add the cream just before serving, along with salt and pepper. Turn up
heat for a moment, but do not boil. Stir again and serve.

Serves 4

PAPAS Y CEBOLLAS
MASHED POTATOES AND ONIONS

6 medium potatoes, pared and cut into ½-inch dice
4 medium onions, coarsely chopped
3 cloves garlic, quartered
Salt and freshly ground pepper to taste
1 can (4 ounces) chopped green chilies, drained
½ cup milk

1. Place the potatoes, onions, and garlic in a saucepan with water to cover. Salt and pepper generously. Bring to a boil; reduce the heat and simmer, covered, for 20 minutes. Drain, saving a little of the cooking liquid.
2. Mash the potatoes, onions, and garlic well, adding a little cooking liquid to moisten. Add the milk and mash again to a smooth purée. Add the chilies and mix thoroughly. Taste and adjust seasoning.

Serves 6

CALABACITAS RELLENAS
STUFFED ZUCCHINI

12 small or 6 medium zucchini
½ pound Monterey Jack, mild white cheddar, or Muenster cheese, cut in thin strips
½ cup cooked or canned corn kernels
2 eggs, separated
1 teaspoon salt
½ teaspoon freshly ground pepper
½ teaspoon dried oregano
2 tablespoons all-purpose flour
Salt and freshly ground pepper to taste
Peanut, corn, or safflower oil for frying

1. In water to cover, parboil all the whole zucchini for 5 minutes. Cut each in half lengthwise and carefully scrape out the seeds with a spoon. In the hollows of each half, lay strips of cheese and some corn kernels; sprinkle with salt, pepper, and oregano. Fasten the halves together with toothpicks.
2. Beat the egg whites until very stiff. Still beating, add the egg yolks, one at a time. Beat in the flour, salt, and pepper.
3. Heat oil about ½-inch deep in a skillet or sauté pan. When at the smoking point, dip each zucchini in the egg batter and fry, 2 at a time, until browned. Keep warm in a low oven until all zucchini are fried. Remove toothpicks before serving.

Serves 6

CHAYOTES RELLENOS
STUFFED CHAYOTES

3 chayotes, halved and seeded
2 tablespoons butter
1 medium onion, minced
Salt and freshly ground pepper to taste
½ cup fresh bread crumbs
¼ cup grated Parmesan cheese

1. Cook the chayotes in boiling water for about 45 minutes. Drain. When cool enough to handle, scoop out the pulp, leaving the shell intact. Mash the pulp with a fork and set aside.
2. Preheat the oven to 350°F.
3. In a skillet, melt the butter and sauté the onion until golden. Stir in the chayote pulp, salt, and pepper and cook over low heat for 2 or 3 minutes.
4. Stuff the chayote shells with the chayote-onion mixture. Combine the bread crumbs and Parmesan and top each chayote half generously with the mixture.
5. Set the chayote halves on a baking sheet and bake until the crumbs are browned, or run under the broiler until golden. (Do not eat the shells—they are merely decorative.)

VARIATION: Mix chayote pulp with leftover picadillo, chicken, or pork; mince the meat, sauté with the onion and chayote pulp, and stuff the shells. This makes a nice luncheon main dish.

Serves 6

ESPARRAGOS EN SALSA ALMENDRA
ASPARAGUS IN ALMOND SAUCE

1 pound fresh asparagus, with woody ends snapped off
4 tablespoons butter
½ cup toasted almonds or walnuts, chopped
½ cup fresh bread crumbs
Salt and freshly ground pepper to taste

1. In a skillet, cook the asparagus in a little water until just tender, 8 to 10 minutes. Drain.
2. Melt the butter in a small skillet and stir in the nuts, bread crumbs, salt, and pepper. Stir and toss until the bread crumbs are browned. Serve over the hot asparagus.

VARIATION: The nut sauce made with walnuts is also delicious over tender-crisp string beans or cauliflower.

Serves 6

ESCABECHE DE CHILES MORRONES
RED BELL PEPPERS WITH VINEGAR AND OIL

6 red bell peppers, roasted, peeled, seeded, and deveined
½ cup light Italian olive oil
6 cloves garlic, quartered
1 large onion, halved and thinly sliced
¼ cup mild white vinegar
1 teaspoon dried oregano
Salt and freshly ground pepper

1. Cut the peppers in quarters. Set aside.
2. Heat the oil in a skillet and sauté the garlic and onion until the onion is wilted. Add the peppers and cook 2 or 3 minutes.
3. Remove the vegetables from the heat. Let cool slightly, then stir in the vinegar, oregano, salt, and pepper. Serve at room temperature or—better still—allow to marinate in the refrigerator and serve slightly chilled.

Serves 4–6

CHILES RELLENOS DE QUESO
CHILIES STUFFED WITH CHEESE

Follow the recipe for Chiles Rellenos (page 78). Stuff the chilies with thin slices of Monterey Jack cheese (about ¼ pound total) instead of *picadillo*, and proceed with the recipe.

CHILES RELLENOS DE ELOTE
CHILIES STUFFED WITH CORN

THE STUFFING:
3 cups canned Green Giant Corn, drained or any canned corn, very well drained or cooked kernels from 3 ears of fresh corn
2 cloves garlic
½ teaspoon salt
1 tablespoon peanut, corn, or safflower oil
1 tablespoon butter
1 large onion, chopped
1 large fresh, ripe tomato, peeled, seeded, and chopped
Freshly ground pepper to taste
½ teaspoon dried oregano
1½ cups shredded Monterey Jack cheese

125

THE CHILIES:

  6 *chiles poblanos* (California, Anaheim, Güero), prepared as in Chiles
    Rellenos (page 78)

THE SAUCE:

  2 tablespoons butter
  2 tablespoons all-purpose flour
  1½ cups milk
  ½ teaspoon salt
  ¼ teaspoon white pepper
  ½ cup shredded Monterey Jack cheese
  ¼ cup grated Parmesan cheese

1. Heat the oil in a large skillet and sauté the garlic and onion with ½ tea-spoon salt until the onion is translucent and limp. Add the tomato, corn kernels, pepper, and oregano. Simmer for 5 minutes. Remove from the heat and stir in the 1½ cups cheese. Set aside.

2. Preheat the oven to 350°F.

3. Stuff the chilies with the corn mixture and place in a shallow baking dish.

4. Melt the butter in a saucepan; stir in the flour. Add the milk gradually, stirring until smooth. Raise the heat and cook, stirring, until the sauce boils and thickens. Stir in ½ teaspoon salt, white pepper, and ½ cup Monterey Jack cheese. Keep stirring until the cheese melts and is incorporated. Pour over the chilies. Sprinkle with Parmesan and bake for 20 to 30 minutes, or until lightly browned on top.

Serves 6

ENSALADAS: SALADS

You are more likely to find seafood, fish, chicken, mixed-vegetable, and meat salads in Mexico than you are to find green salads. Delicious Mexican salads, such as Escabeche (Marinated Fish, page 130), Carne a la Vinegreta (Marinated Meat Salad, page 130), and Ensalada de Pollo y Chiles Verdes (Chicken and Green Chili Salad, page 131), are served as main courses, rather than as sides dishes. You may, of course, serve smaller portions of these salads at luncheons, or as part of a varied salad plate. Or allow guests to help themselves to salads at a buffet table. (Green salads have only recently become popular in Mexico, as modern Mexicans are embracing some food fashions of the United States and Europe.)

ENSALADA DE COLIFLOR
CAULIFLOWER SALAD

1 small head cauliflower
½ pound mustard greens, tough stems removed, leaves rinsed well, then torn in shreds
2 tablespoons orange juice
1 egg yolk
6 tablespoons light Italian olive oil
2 tablespoons mild white vinegar
1 fresh *chile jalapeño*, seeded and minced
½ teaspoon dried oregano
Salt and freshly ground pepper to taste

1. Cook the cauliflower in a small amount of boiling water until just tender. Drain in a colander and cool. (You may also use raw cauliflower.)
2. Separate the cauliflower into flowerets. Combine with the mustard greens in a salad bowl.
3. In a small bowl whisk together the egg yolk and orange juice; add the oil slowly, beating as you do so. Add the vinegar, still beating. Whisk in the rest of the ingredients and pour over the cauliflower and mustard greens. Toss to blend.

Serves 6

ENSALADA DE COLIFLOR Y AGUACATE
SALAD OF CAULIFLOWER AND GUACAMOLE

1 small cauliflower
¼ cup mild white vinegar
Guacamole (page 38)
½ cup grated Parmesan cheese

1. Cook the cauliflower with the vinegar in salted water to cover until just tender. Cool and break into flowerets.
2. Combine the cauliflower with the Guacamole and sprinkle with grated Parmesan. Serve as an appetizer or luncheon main dish.

Serves 6

ENSALADA DE NOPALITOS
CACTUS SALAD

2 cans (10 ounces each) *nopalitos* (nopal cactus pieces)
1 pound fresh, ripe tomatoes, cut in eighths
1 medium onion, chopped
1 tablespoon chopped coriander leaves
1 *chile serrano* or *jalapeño* (fresh or canned), seeded and chopped
¾ cup oil and vinegar dressing (3 parts oil to 1 part vinegar)
½ cup crumbled farmer or feta cheese (optional)

Drain and rinse the cactus pieces. Combine with the tomatoes, onion, coriander, and chili. Toss in dressing and serve sprinkled with crumbled cheese.

Serves 6

ENSALADA DE PAPAS
POTATO SALAD

3 pounds boiling potatoes, in their skins
1 large Bermuda onion, finely chopped
2 teaspoons salt
1 teaspoon freshly ground pepper
3 tablespoons chopped fresh parsley
1 can (4 ounces) chopped green chilies, undrained
1 tablespoon dry mustard
½ cup cold water
1½ cups mayonnaise

1. Wash potatoes thoroughly; place in a large saucepan and cover with water. Bring to a boil; reduce the heat and simmer, covered, for 25 minutes, or until the potatoes are tender but still firm. Drain and cool.

2. When the potatoes are cool enough to handle, peel them and slice them crosswise into ⅛-inch rounds. Place in a large bowl with the onion, salt, pepper, parsley, and green chilies.

3. In a small bowl, whisk the mustard and water until dissolved. Gradually whisk in the mayonnaise until the dressing is smooth. Pour over the potatoes and mix gently and thoroughly with a wooden spoon. As you mix, break up some of the potatoes for a creamier texture. Chill before serving.

NOTE: This salad is even better tasting when it is made 24 hours or more ahead of time.

Serves 8

JÍCAMA PICO DE GALLO
JÍCAMA SALAD

2 cups peeled jícama, cut into ¼- or ½-inch dice
1 red bell pepper, seeded, deveined, and cut into ½-inch dice
1 small onion, halved and thinly sliced
1 cup diced cucumber
2 navel oranges, peeled, sectioned, and chopped
¼ cup light Italian olive oil
2 tablespoons lime juice
½ teaspoon dried oregano or 1 tablespoon finely chopped coriander leaves
Salt and cayenne pepper to taste

Combine the vegetables in a bowl. Pour the oil and lime juice over them and toss with oregano or coriander, salt, and cayenne. Chill.

Serves 4–6

ENSALADA DE NOCHE BUENA
CHRISTMAS EVE SALAD

3 beets, cooked and chopped
3 oranges, peeled and sectioned
1½ cups peeled, diced (¼- to ½-inch) jícama
3 bananas, peeled and sliced
3 slices fresh pineapple, cut into small chunks
3 limes, peeled and thinly sliced
Shredded lettuce
½ cup chopped dry-roasted peanuts
Seeds of 1 pomegranate

¼ cup sugar or 1 piece (4 inches) sugar cane, pared and chopped (both
  optional)
¾ cup salad oil or light Italian olive oil
¼ cup red or white wine vinegar
Salt

  1. Mix the beets, oranges, jícama, bananas, pineapple, and limes together
and chill.
  2. Line a salad bowl with the lettuce. Fill the lettuce with chilled fruits.
Sprinkle with peanuts, pomegranate seeds, and sugar or sugar cane. Just
before serving, mix the oil, vinegar, and salt and drizzle over the salad.

Serves 6–8

ESCABECHE
MARINATED FISH

1½ pounds any firm-fleshed fish fillets
2 tablespoons light Italian olive oil
1 large onion, halved and thinly sliced
3 cloves garlic, thinly sliced
3 canned peeled green chilies, drained, seeded and coarsely chopped
½ cup mild white vinegar
½ teaspoon ground cumin
1 teaspoon salt
Freshly ground pepper to taste
Juice of 1 orange
Shredded lettuce, capers, and sliced hard-cooked eggs for garnish

  1. Heat the olive oil in a skillet and sauté the fillets until lightly browned.
Remove with a slotted spoon and slice into 1-inch strips. Arrange the fish
in a shallow serving dish.
  2. In the oil remaining in the pan, sauté the onion and garlic until just
wilted. Add the green chilies, vinegar, cumin, salt, pepper, and orange juice.
Heat through and pour over the fish strips.
  3. Chill *escabeche* for 1 hour or more. Serve with garnishes, passed separately.

Serves 6

CARNE A LA VINEGRETA
MARINATED MEAT SALAD

The meat in this recipe must marinate 3 hours or more.

1½ pounds cooked roast beef, tongue, lean pork, or steak, cut into thin
  strips (about 3 cups)

1 large onion, halved and thinly sliced
2 tablespoons capers
2 tablespoons chopped coriander leaves
½ cup light Italian olive oil
⅓ cup red or white wine vinegar
1 teaspoon dried oregano
¼ teaspoon cayenne pepper
1 tablespoon Dijon mustard
½ teaspoon salt
Romaine lettuce leaves, shredded

1. Place the meat strips in a shallow bowl. Cover with a layer of sliced onion. Sprinkle with capers and coriander.

2. Mix together the oil, vinegar, oregano, cayenne, mustard, and salt. Whisk well and pour over the meat and onions.

3. Cover the meat tightly with plastic wrap and allow to marinate in the refrigerator for 3 hours or overnight. Before serving, toss the salad and place on shredded romaine lettuce.

Serves 6

ENSALADA DE POLLO Y CHILES VERDES
CHICKEN AND GREEN CHILI SALAD

The chicken in this recipe must marinate for several hours.

3 whole chicken breasts, poached, skinned, boned, then halved and cut
    into ½-inch cubes
1 medium onion, chopped
1 clove garlic, minced
2 tablespoons chopped coriander leaves
3 canned peeled green chilies, drained, seeded, and cut crosswise into ½-
    inch rings
1½ cups mayonnaise
1 tablespoon Dijon mustard
2 dashes Maggi seasoning
Salt and freshly ground pepper to taste
½ pound fresh mushrooms, sliced
Romaine lettuce leaves, shredded

1. Place all the ingredients (except the mushrooms and lettuce) in a bowl and toss gently but thoroughly. Chill for several hours.

2. Just before serving, fold in the sliced mushrooms; transfer to a serving bowl. Arrange shredded lettuce around the rim. Sprinkle with additional chopped coriander, if you like.

Serves 6

ENSALADA DE ATÚN
TUNA SALAD

Use as a sandwich filling, appetizer, or luncheon main dish.

1 can (6½ ounces) solid white tuna, drained and flaked
1 small onion, finely chopped
1 cup chopped raw cabbage
4 canned *chiles serranos en escabeche*, finely chopped
1 level teaspoon freshly ground pepper
1½ cups mayonnaise (or to taste)

Toss the first 5 ingredients thoroughly; add the mayonnaise and mix thoroughly.

SUGGESTION: As a main dish, garnish with radishes, olives, tomatoes, quartered hard-cooked eggs, and lettuce.

Serves 4–6

ENSALADA DE CAMARÓNES
SHRIMP SALAD

1 pound shrimp, cooked, peeled and cut in pieces
1 can (14 ounces) artichoke hearts, drained and quartered
3 scallions, with greens, chopped
1 fresh, ripe tomato, peeled and cubed
2 tablespoons chopped coriander leaves
¼ cup sliced pimiento-stuffed green olives
3 *chiles jalapeños* (fresh or canned), seeded, deveined, and chopped
Freshly ground pepper
1½ cups mayonnaise

Toss all the ingredients in a salad bowl until mayonnaise is evenly distributed. Chill before serving.

VARIATION: Substitute 1 large, ripe avocado for the artichoke hearts. Peel, cube, and toss gently with the other ingredients.

Serves 6

CAMARÓNES A LA BANDERA
RED, WHITE, AND GREEN CONFETTI SHRIMP SALAD

½ cup mayonnaise
½ cup sour cream or *crème fraîche*
3 cups cooked medium shrimp, shelled, deveined, and cut into small
  pieces
1 medium onion, chopped
1 fresh *chile jalapeño*, seeded, deveined, and finely chopped
6 small new potatoes, cooked in their skins and sliced
1 cup unpeeled cucumber, diced
3 hard-cooked eggs, chopped
½ teaspoon cayenne pepper
Salt and freshly ground pepper to taste
1 red bell pepper, seeded, deveined, and cut into ½-inch dice

1. Mix the mayonnaise and sour cream together.
2. Combine the rest of the ingredients (except the diced red pepper); fold
in the mayonnaise mixture and toss well. Taste for seasoning. Arrange in a
glass bowl and sprinkle with the diced red pepper.

Serves 6

POSTRES: DESSERTS

Fresh fruit is the national dessert of Mexico—along with the inevitable *flan* of the Spaniards. Mexicans do have a prodigious sweet tooth, however, so it was fated that cakes, all manner of puddings, and cookies should enter their dessert mix. *Ates,* or fruit pastes, are popular in Mexican restaurants in this country, with guava paste (served with saltines and cream cheese) taking the lead. Cakes are often nut-based tortes—wheat not being that popular in colonial times—with icings and fillings of chocolate, brown sugar, vanilla, and fruit flavors (the favorite). As in countries such as Switzerland, cakes are usually bought at a bakery rather than baked at home. But home bakers are again beginning to produce varied, unusual, and mouth-watering desserts.

PASTEL DE CHOCOLATE MEXICANO
MEXICAN CHOCOLATE CAKE

Butter and all-purpose flour for greasing and flouring pan
4 ounces semisweet chocolate
2 tablespoons rum or Kahlúa
¼ pound (1 stick) sweet butter, at room temperature
½ cup sugar
2 teaspoons ground cinnamon
4 eggs, separated
1 cup finely ground almonds

1. Butter and flour an 8-inch round × 1½-inch deep cake pan. Set aside.
2. Melt the chocolate with rum or Kahlúa in a small saucepan over low heat.
3. Preheat the oven to 350°F.
4. In the large bowl of an electric mixer, cream the butter; add the sugar gradually. Add the cinnamon and beat until thoroughly combined. Beat in the egg yolks, one at a time, until well blended.
5. In a separate bowl, beat the egg whites until they form stiff peaks.
6. With a rubber spatula, blend the melted chocolate and rum into the butter and sugar mixture, then fold in the almonds. (The mixture will be thick.) Thoroughly stir in one-third of the beaten egg whites, then gradually and gently fold in the rest of the egg whites until all are thoroughly mixed.
7. Pour the batter into the prepared pan and bake for 25 to 30 minutes. Remove from the oven and allow the pan to cool on a rack for about 10 minutes. To remove the cake from the pan, run a knife around the edge of the pan; cover the pan with a rack or serving plate and invert the cake onto the flat surface.

SUGGESTION: Cake may be served with whipped cream, flavored with rum or Kahlúa on the side.

NOTE: This is a dense and moist cake and needs no icing.

Serves 8

PASTEL DE NUEZ
NUT TORTE

Butter and all-purpose flour for greasing and flouring pan
¾ cup unbleached all-purpose flour
1 teaspoon baking powder
3 eggs, separated
½ cup granulated sugar
1 cup finely ground pecans or walnuts
¼ pound (1 stick) sweet butter, clarified (see below)
1 tablespoon vanilla extract
Confectioners sugar for dusting

1. Preheat the oven to 350°F.
2. Butter and flour an 8-inch round × 1½-inch deep cake pan. Set aside.
3. Sift the flour and baking powder together. Set aside.
4. Beat the egg yolks with the granulated sugar until light and fluffy. Gradually add the flour mixture. Stir in the ground nuts. Add the clarified butter, taking care not to add the milky residue in the bottom of the pan. Add the vanilla.
5. Beat the egg whites until stiff peaks form. Fold one-third of the whites into the batter to lighten it, then fold in the rest of the whites, gently but thoroughly. Pour the batter into the prepared cake pan and bake for about 30 minutes.
6. Remove the cake from the oven and allow to cool in the pan on a rack for about 10 minutes. To remove the cake from the pan, run a knife around the edge of the pan; cover the pan with a rack or serving plate and invert the cake onto the flat surface.
7. Dust the top of the cake with confectioners sugar.

To clarify butter: Melt the butter slowly in a small saucepan. Allow to stand until the milky sediment settles to the bottom of the pan.

VARIATION: Omit confectioners sugar and serve the cake spread with ½ cup of mango or apricot preserves cooked for several minutes with 2 tablespoons granulated sugar. Spread the preserves over the cake while it is still warm. Decorate the edge of the cake with evenly spaced whole nut meats, if you like.

Serves 8

PASTEL MEXICANO DE QUESO FRESCA
MEXICAN CHEESE CAKE

1 cup crushed chocolate wafers
3 tablespoons melted butter
2 pounds cream cheese, at room temperature
4 eggs
1½ cups granulated sugar
¼ cup Kahlúa or other coffee liqueur
1 teaspoon ground cinnamon
Confectioners sugar and powdered cocoa for dusting

1. Preheat the oven to 350°F.
2. In a bowl, combine the chocolate wafer crumbs and melted butter. Press the mixture evenly into the bottom and part way up the sides of an 8-inch round × 3-inch deep metal cake pan. Bake the shell for 8 to 10 minutes, until it is set; take care that it does not burn. Set aside to cool while preparing the batter.
3. Reduce oven temperature to 325°F.
4. Place the cream cheese, eggs, sugar, Kahlúa, and cinnamon in the large bowl of an electric mixer; start beating at low speed; increase the speed to high and beat until the ingredients are thoroughly blended and smooth. Pour the batter into chocolate shell and tilt slightly to make sure the mixture is level.
5. Set the pan in a larger pan and pour boiling water into the outer pan to a depth of 1 inch. Do not let the edges of the pans touch. Set the pans on the center rack of the oven and bake for 1½ to 2 hours. Turn off the oven heat and allow the cake to sit in the oven for 30 minutes longer.
6. Remove the cake pan from the water bath and place on a rack to cool to room temperature.
7. To remove the cake from the pan, run a metal spatula or sharp knife around the edge of the cake; place a round plate over the cake and carefully invert. Remove the cake pan and place a serving plate over the now upside-down cake and invert again so the cake is right side up on the serving plate.
8. Dust the top of the cake with a mixture of confectioners sugar and powdered cocoa.

Serves 8

PUDÍN DE GARBANZO
GARBANZO BEAN CAKE

This is an unusual, tightly textured, puddinglike cake that can be served with fresh fruit or ice cream.

1 cup dried garbanzo beans (chick-peas)
4 eggs
1 cup sugar
½ teaspoon baking powder

Grated rind of 1 lemon
Butter for greasing pan
Juice of 1 lemon
Confectioners sugar

1. Soak the garbanzos in water to cover overnight.
2. Rinse the beans and place them in a saucepan; cover with salted water and bring to a boil. Reduce the heat to a simmer and cook the beans gently until tender (1 to 2 hours).
3. Wash the cooked beans in a sieve or colander under cold water. Place in the workbowl of a food processor fitted with the steel blade and purée. Add the 4 eggs, sugar, baking powder, and lemon rind to the purée and pulse a few times to combine well.
4. Preheat the oven to 350°F.
5. Butter a 9-inch round cake pan. Cut a round of wax paper to fit in the pan bottom, set it in place, and butter the top side. Pour the batter in to the cake pan.
6. Bake the cake for 45 minutes, or until a knife inserted in the center comes out dry. Cool on a rack for 15 minutes, then remove from the pan and cool to room temperature. Before serving, squeeze the lemon juice over the cake and sprinkle with confectioners sugar.

VARIATIONS: Purée the garbanzos with ½ cup evaporated milk. Separate the eggs. Add the yolks with the sugar, baking powder, and lemon rind. Beat the whites separately until soft peaks form; fold into the batter. Pour into an angel-food pan and bake at 350°F for 1 hour and 10 minutes. Test with a toothpick or knife before removing from the oven to cool.

A cup of raisins, glazed fruits, nuts, or chocolate bits may be added to the batter. If you add chocolate, eliminate the lemon rind and juice. Substitute a sprinkling of cinnamon-sugar for the confectioners sugar.

Serves 8

ROLLO DE CALABAZA RELLENO CON CREMA DE JENJIBRE
PUMPKIN GINGER CREAM LOG

THE LOG:
Butter and flour for greasing and flouring pan
5 eggs, separated
¾ cup granulated sugar
1 cup pumpkin purée (solid-pack pumpkin)
¼ cup all-purpose flour
1 teaspoon baking powder
1 teaspoon ground ginger
1 teaspoon ground cinnamon
½ teaspoon ground cloves or allspice

Pinch of grated nutmeg
⅛ teaspoon salt
⅛ teaspoon cream of tartar
Confectioners sugar

THE FILLING:
1½ cups heavy cream
2 tablespoons confectioners sugar
1 cup crystallized ginger, coarsely chopped

1. Preheat the oven to 350°F.
2. Butter a jelly-roll pan, 16×11 inches; line it with waxed paper; butter and lightly flour the paper.
3. Sift the flour with the baking powder.
4. In a large bowl with an electric mixer, beat the egg yolks at high speed for about 3 minutes, until they are frothy. Gradually add ½ cup of the granulated sugar and continue to beat the mixture for several minutes, until it ribbons when the beater is lifted. On low speed, fold in the pumpkin, flour mixture, ginger, cinnamon, cloves, and nutmeg. Beat just until all ingredients are combined. Set aside.
5. In a separate bowl, using the mixer at high speed, beat the egg whites with the salt and cream of tartar until they hold soft peaks. Gradually beat in the remaining ¼ cup granulated sugar, one tablespoon at a time, and beat the whites until they hold stiff peaks.
6. With a rubber spatula, fold one-fourth of the whites into the pumpkin mixture, gently but thoroughly. Fold the remaining whites into the mixture until there are no traces of white. Pour the batter into the lined jelly-roll pan and spread evenly with a spatula. Bake for 20 minutes, or until the cake shrinks from the sides of the pan. Cool for 30 minutes, then invert onto a clean sheet of waxed paper lightly sprinkled with confectioners sugar. Carefully peel the waxed paper from the inverted cake.
7. In a chilled bowl, beat the heavy cream until it thickens. Add the 2 tablespoons confectioners sugar and continue to beat until the cream holds stiff peaks. Fold in the crystallized ginger.
8. Spread the filling mixture evenly over the cake and roll it tightly, lengthwise, lifting the waxed paper with it to help you roll, and transfer to a serving platter. Remove the waxed paper carefully; sprinkle the log with additional confectioners sugar.

NOTE: This dessert is better if it is chilled for several hours before serving.

Serves 8–10

FLAN DE KAHLÚA

This dessert must be refrigerated for several hours before serving.

1½ cups sugar
½ cup water
4 cups milk
12 egg yolks

1 whole egg
½ teaspoon ground cinnamon
¼ cup Kahlúa

1. Preheat the oven to 350°F.
2. Combine ¾ cup of the sugar and the water in a small, heavy saucepan and cook over low heat, without stirring, until the sugar is dissolved and the syrup turns amber brown.
3. Pour syrup into a 1½-quart ring mold, tilting and turning the mold to coat the bottom and sides. Set aside to cool.
4. In a saucepan, bring the milk to just under a boil.
5. In a bowl, beat the egg yolks and egg; add the remaining ¾ cup sugar and beat until thoroughly blended. Add the hot milk, whisking continuously; add the cinnamon and Kahlúa.
6. Place the caramel-coated mold in a larger baking pan. Carefully pour the custard mixture into the ring mold. Place the pans in the center of the oven and pour hot water into the larger pan about halfway up the sides of the ring mold. Bake for 1 hour or until a knife inserted into the center of the custard comes out clean. Remove the mold from the pan of water and place on a rack to cool.
7. Refrigerate the mold 2 or 3 hours or overnight before serving. To unmold, run a knife around the edge; cover the mold with a round serving plate and quickly invert. Place the mold on a flat surface and tap gently around to release the custard. Lift off the mold. Cut the custard into slices and spoon the caramel sauce over them to serve.

VARIATION: To make plain *flan*, substitute 1 tablespoon vanilla for the Kahlúa.

Serves 8

FLAN DE PACANAS
CUSTARD WITH GROUND PECANS

This dessert must be refrigerated for several hours before serving.

1¾ cups sugar
6 eggs
2 teaspoons vanilla extract
3 cups milk
1 cup ground pecans
½ teaspoon ground cinnamon

1. In a small saucepan, heat 1 cup of the sugar over low heat until a golden syrup forms. Pour the caramel into an 8-inch round × 2-inch deep pan and tip to coat the bottom and sides of the pan.
2. Preheat the oven to 350°F.
3. Beat the eggs with the remaining ¾ cup sugar; add the vanilla. Stir in the milk and mix well. Stir in the nuts and cinnamon. Pour the mixture into the caramel-coated pan.

4. Place the pan in a larger pan and pour boiling water into the larger pan halfway up the sides of the smaller pan. Bake for 50 minutes, or until the custard is firm. Chill for several hours.

4. To unmold, run a knife around the edge of the *flan*, place a serving dish over the pan, and invert. The *flan* and the caramel sauce should now be on the serving dish.

VARIATIONS: For Flan de Nuez (Nut Flan), substitute walnuts, almonds (use almond extract to replace the vanilla), or hazelnuts for the pecans.

For Flan de Café (Coffee Flan), mix 2 teaspoons instant coffee with just enough hot water to melt the crystals. Combine with the milk; proceed with the recipe.

Serves 6

PUDÍN DE NUEZ
ELEGANT NUT PUDDING

1 can (14 ounces) sweetened condensed milk
3¼ cups whole milk
6 eggs
3 ounces pecans or walnuts, chopped
1 tablespoon vanilla extract
⅛ teaspoon baking soda

1. Place all the ingredients in a blender or the workbowl of a food processor fitted with the steel blade. Process until combined and smooth.
2. Pour the mixture into the saucepan and stir over moderate heat until it just begins to boil.
3. Remove the pan from the heat and stir to blend thoroughly. Cool slightly and pour into a lightly oiled 6-cup decorative mold. Refrigerate for several hours.
4. To unmold, run a knife around the edge of the *flan*, place a serving dish over the pan, and invert.

Serves 6–8

CAPIROTADA
BREAD PUDDING

½ pound French bread
4 tablespoons butter, melted
½ cup raisins (optional)
½ cup slivered almonds
4 cups milk

1 cup (packed) brown sugar
1 cinnamon stick
1 tablespoon vanilla extract
3 whole eggs
3 egg yolks
1 cup heavy cream
¼ cup dark rum or Kahlúa

1. Preheat the oven to 375°F.
2. Cut the bread on the diagonal into ¼-inch slices. Brush one side of each slice with melted butter and bake on a cookie sheet for about 10 minutes, turning once, until crisp and golden brown. (Do not burn.)
3. Arrange the bread slices, overlapping, in a 1½-quart baking dish, preferably oval shaped and 1½- to 2-inches deep. Sprinkle the bread with the raisins and almonds.
4. In a saucepan, bring the milk, sugar, and cinnamon stick to a boil; stir until the sugar is dissolved. Add the vanilla, then remove from the heat; let cool slightly.
5. In a bowl, beat the whole eggs and yolks; add the cream and rum. Pour the egg mixture into the cooled milk and sugar mixture; stir. Pour the liquid over the bread in the baking dish.
6. Carefully place baking dish into a larger baking pan and place on the bottom rack of the oven. Pour boiling water into the larger pan to a depth of 1 inch. Bake until the custard is set, or about 35 to 40 minutes. To test for doneness, insert a knife into the custard. If it comes out clean, the custard is done. Remove the baking dish from the larger pan of water and place on a rack to cool. Serve warm or at room temperature with Caramel Syrup (recipe below).

Serves 8

MIEL DE CARAMELO
CARAMEL SYRUP

1 cup sugar
1 cup water
Grated zest of 1 orange

1. Combine the sugar and ½ cup of the water in a saucepan and bring to a boil. Cook over moderately high heat until the sugar starts to turn golden. Reduce the heat and add the grated orange zest; continue cooking, watching carefully, until the syrup is dark brown. Remove the pan from the heat immediately.
2. Carefully add the remaining ½ cup water to the syrup. Return to the heat and cook, stirring, until the syrup is thin and smooth.

Makes about ¾ cup

POSTRE DE MANGO
CHILLED MANGO DESSERT

This dessert must be chilled thoroughly before serving.

1 envelope unflavored gelatin
1 large can (32 ounces) mango slices, drained (liquid reserved)
1 can (14 ounces) sweetened condensed milk
¼ cup dark rum
Juice of 1 lime

    1. Put the gelatin and ¼ cup of reserved mango liquid in a small bowl and stir until the gelatin is softened. Set the bowl in a basin of simmering water and stir until the gelatin is dissolved. Set aside.
    2. Combine the mangos, condensed milk, rum, and lime juice in a blender or food processor fitted with the steel blade. Add the gelatin mixture and blend. Spoon the liquid into individual serving cups and chill completely before serving.

SUGGESTION: Purée 1 pint of fresh strawberries and spoon over the top of the mango dessert.

Serves 6

PASTEL DE MANGO
MANGO PIE

1 large can (32 ounces) mango slices, drained
¼ cup dark rum
½ cup sugar
3 tablespoons all-purpose flour
½ teaspoon ground cinnamon
Pastry for one 9-inch pie crust, plus extra pastry for lattice strips
1 tablespoon butter

    1. Marinate the mango slices in rum for 30 minutes.
    2. Preheat the oven to 425°F.
    3. Mix together the sugar, flour, and cinnamon and combine with the mango slices and rum. Arrange in the prepared, unbaked pie crust; dot with butter and place lattice strips over the fruit.
    4. Bake on the center rack of the oven for 45 to 50 minutes. Cool.

SUGGESTION: Mango pie is delicious served with whipped cream or vanilla ice cream.

Serves 6–8

PASTELITOS DE BODA
MEXICAN WEDDING CAKES

¼ pound (1 stick) sweet butter, at room temperature
½ cup plus 2 tablespoons confectioners sugar
1 teaspoon vanilla extract
1 cup sifted all-purpose flour
1 cup finely chopped pecans or walnuts

1. Preheat the oven to 375°F.
2. In the bowl of an electric mixer, cream the butter. Add the 2 tablespoons confectioners sugar and the vanilla and beat for 1 minute on low speed. Add the flour and pecans, beating only until thoroughly mixed.
3. Shape the dough into balls, using a scant tablespoon of dough for each cookie. Place the cookies 1 inch apart on an unbuttered cookie sheet. Bake for 15 minutes, until lightly browned. Transfer to a rack to cool. Roll the warm cookies in the ½ cup confectioners sugar.

Makes about 2 dozen cookies

PLÁTANOS FRITOS
FRIED GLAZED PLANTAINS (OR BANANAS)

4 very ripe plantains or 4 firm bananas, peeled and cut in half lengthwise
4 tablespoons butter
1 cup (packed) dark brown sugar
¼ cup dark rum
½ teaspoon grated nutmeg
Grated zest of 1 orange

Heat the butter in a skillet and add the plantains or bananas. Cook over low heat until tender, turning once. Sprinkle with the sugar, rum, nutmeg, and orange zest. Simmer until the sugar is completely melted. Spoon the syrup over the plantains and cook a few minutes more. Serve hot, 2 halves per serving.

VARIATION: Combine ½ cup sour cream or *crème fraîche* with a little powdered sugar to taste. Top each serving with a dollop.

Serves 4

BUÑUELOS
FRITTERS IN ANISE-FLAVORED SYRUP

THE FRITTERS:
 1 cup water
 1 teaspoon anise seeds
 3½ cups all-purpose flour
 1 teaspoon baking powder
 ½ teaspoon salt
 3 eggs
 1 cup corn or safflower oil

1. Boil the water with the anise seeds for a few minutes. Strain and discard the seeds. Set the water aside to cool.

2. Sift the flour with the baking powder and salt. Add the eggs and enough anise water to make a firm dough. Knead until quite smooth.

3. Divide the dough into about 20 pieces. Wet hands and roll each piece into a ball. Flatten each ball and press a hole in the center. Place the buñuelos on a floured surface and allow to dry for about 30 minutes.

4. In a heavy skillet or saucepan, heat the oil to the smoking point and drop in the buñuelos. Fry, a few at a time, until puffy and golden on both sides. Remove from the oil with a slotted spoon and drain on paper towels. Serve with Anise Syrup (recipe below).

Makes 20

THE SYRUP:
 1 pound dark brown sugar
 1 cup water
 1 teaspoon anise seeds

In a saucepan, dissolve the sugar in water. Add the anise seeds and bring to a boil. Boil until the syrup thickens. Remove from the heat. Pour through a sieve to remove the seeds. Cool.

NOTE: The anise seeds produce a traditional flavor but may be eliminated.

VARIATION: Place 1 cup sugar, 1 teaspoon ground cinnamon, and ¼ teaspoon ground cloves in a paper bag. When the buñuelos are drained but still warm, shake them in the bag, one at a time, to coat.

Makes about 1½ cups

PUDÍN DE ARROZ
"DRUNKEN" RICE PUDDING

This dessert must be chilled thoroughly before serving.

 1 cup water
 Pinch of salt

1 tablespoon julienned or grated lemon zest
1 cup long-grain rice (unconverted)
4 cups milk
2 egg yolks
1 cup (packed) brown sugar
½ cup raisins soaked in ¼ cup rum or tequila
Ground cinnamon

1. In a saucepan, bring the water to a boil. Add the salt, lemon zest, and rice and boil slowly, stirring occasionally, until the water is absorbed.

2. Add 3¾ cups of the milk to the rice and bring to a boil again. Continue to boil until the mixture becomes thick and the rice is soft. Stir often to prevent sticking.

3. Beat the egg yolks with the remaining ¼ cup milk. Mix the beaten yolks, sugar, and raisins with their soaking liquid into the rice. Bring to a boil. Stir to incorporate the ingredients; continue to cook 1 or 2 minutes more.

4. Pour into a 2-quart greased mold or baking dish. Chill thoroughly. Serve sprinkled with cinnamon.

Serves 8

MERENGUES
MERINGUES

2 egg whites
½ cup sugar
⅛ teaspoon salt
¼ teaspoon cream of tartar
½ teaspoon vanilla or almond extract

1. Preheat the oven to 250°F.

2. By hand or with an electric mixer, beat the egg whites till foamy. Gradually add the rest of the ingredients, beating vigorously, until the whites hold stiff peaks.

3. Drop the meringue mixture by heaping tablespoonfuls onto an *ungreased* cookie sheet. With the back of a spoon, indent the meringue centers to form a bowl or nest. Bake 45 minutes or longer, until dry.

NOTE: Store the meringues in an airtight container. If they soften, heat them again in a very slow oven for a few minutes until crisp.

SUGGESTION: Fill the centers with cooked and chilled fruits, ice cream, fruit custard, chocolate pudding, or mousse.

VARIATION: Add a tablespoon or more of ground almonds, walnuts, or pecans along with the sugar.

Makes 8

CHURROS
CRULLERS

In Mexico, *churros* are often made in one continuous piece and cut into 3-inch lengths when done. They are traditionally served with hot chocolate.

Oil for deep frying
1 lime or lemon, quartered
1 cup water
1 teaspoon salt
1 cup sifted all-purpose flour
½ cup sugar
1 large egg (or 2 small)
Sugar for coating

1. In a deep-fryer or saucepan, heat 2 to 3 inches of oil to high heat and add the lime or lemon quarters.
2. In another saucepan, boil the water. Add the salt, sugar, and flour all at once and immediately begin beating with a wooden spoon. Beat until smooth, then remove from the heat. Beat in the egg and continue to beat until the batter is smooth and shiny.
3. Remove the lime or lemon from the oil. (The oil should be very hot—390°F on a fat thermometer.) Pack the batter into a pastry tube fitted with the star tip and force strips about 3 inches in length into the hot oil a few at a time. Fry until golden. Remove and drain on paper toweling. Sprinkle with or roll in granulated sugar.

VARIATION: Cinnamon may be added to the granulated sugar.

NOTE: If you save the oil, remember that it is flavored with citrus, and is therefore good for deep-frying Shrimp Fritters (page 55), fish, and chicken.

Makes about 1 dozen

BEBIDAS: DRINKS

The celebrity of all Mexican liquors is tequila. It wasn't always the star, though; before Cortés, it did not exist. The Aztecs drank pulque, the undistilled sap of the maguey (also known as the agave, or century plant). Once distilling was introduced to Mexico, after the conquest, the once-popular pulque lost ground to tequila, which is made from distilled maguey.

Tequila is usually colorless, but the brew takes on a yellowish tinge when aged in charred casks. It is traditionally taken neat, accompanied by salt and a section of lime or lemon. The three are combined in the mouth—a tiny bit of salt licked from a mound on the back of the hand, a sip from the glass, and a little lime squeezed through the teeth. There's nothing to prevent you from squeezing the lime into the tequila and rimming the glass with salt, if you like.

One of the most delicious and refreshing of Mexico's exports is its beer. Light or dark, there is something curiously satisfying about it—especially when served with Mexican food. It doesn't hit you over the head with its flavor, yet it holds its own with the most chilied of dishes.

Beer is more appropriate than wine to drink with Mexican food. While Mexico produces wines, its wine industry has not yet caught up with the rest of the world's. Some European or American light white wines do marry well with Mexican foods, but the reds, though more robust, are not suited to the cuisine. Your best bet is to serve beer, fruit juices, or sangría with Mexican meals. Save wine for a subtler cuisine, or for before or after dinner.

After the Spanish introduced the cultivation of sugar cane to Mexico, Mexico began to produce rum. Mexican rums are excellent, but have not been promoted as heavily as another popular drink—Kahlúa, the coffee liqueur.

Mexican soft drinks (refrescos) are of almost endless variety. There are wonderful fruit punches and vegetable juices (jugos), as well as atole, a corn drink made with milk, masa harina, and a favorite flavoring. Herbal teas (tisanes), which are at once delicious, soothing, and curative, are also popular in Mexico, as is the deep, dark coffee drunk throughout the day.

Chocolate was the drink of the Aztec royalty. The Spanish improved on the hot Aztec version by adding sugar, unknown to the Indians. As a hot drink, chocolate became the rage of European capitals; it would be a hundred years before the introduction of the more stimulating coffee and tea dethroned the Mexican sensation.

CAFÉ CON LECHE
COFFEE WITH MILK

Like *café au lait*, Mexican *café con leche* is made from very strong coffee (four times as strong as American coffee) diluted 3 to 1 with hot milk. Mexicans drink *café con leche* for breakfast, and at any time during the day that an eye-opener is needed.

¼ cup drip-grind dark-roast coffee
1 cup water
⅓ cup milk

    1. Brew the coffee as you would regular coffee, using the proportions above.
    2. Heat the milk in a saucepan. Combine with the coffee.

Makes 1 serving; increase
proportionately as needed

CAFÉ DE OLLA
COFFEE MADE IN A POT

This is the after-dinner coffee of Mexico. It is said to be best made in an earthenware pot and served in earthenware cups, but a saucepan (or enameled coffee pot) and regular coffee cups serve just as well. It's what's in the coffee that counts.

4 cups water
½ cup *piloncillo* or dark brown sugar (or to taste)
4 whole cloves
1 cinnamon stick
5 heaping tablespoons all-purpose grind dark-roast coffee

    1. Heat the water with the sugar, cloves, and cinnamon, in a saucepan or enameled coffee pot. Stir until the sugar dissolves, then add the coffee. Bring to a boil; lower the heat and simmer for 2 minutes.
    2. Stir well and cover the pot. Keep warm until the coffee grounds settle to the bottom. Pour through a fine sieve or filter to serve—or pour carefully directly into cups, not disturbing the grounds.

VARIATION: Though not "authentic," a heaping teaspoon of cocoa powder added to the pot with the ground coffee is a delicious variation.

Serves 4

CHOCOLATE
HOT CHOCOLATE (WITH MILK OR WATER)

The chocolate used for chocolate drinks in Mexico is a mixture of chocolate, sugar, cinnamon, and almonds. It is sold in bars sectioned into triangles. Traditionally, Mexican chocolate is made with cold water (the Aztec way)—one triangle to a cup of water—and beaten with one of the oldest of all kitchen utensils, the *molinillo* (a carved, wooden pre-Columbian whisk), which is whirled between the palms until the chocolate dissolves and develops a frothy head.

WITH MILK:
6 ounces Mexican chocolate or unsweetened American chocolate
4 cups whole milk (with ½ teaspoon ground cinnamon and 4 teaspoons sugar added if American chocolate is used)

1. Put the chocolate and milk in a saucepan and bring to a boil, stirring. Remove from the heat and let the bubbling subside.
2. Return to the heat and bring to a boil once more. Remove from the heat and beat with a *molinillo* or wire whisk until frothy, or whirl in a blender or food processor.

WITH WATER:
6 ounces Mexican chocolate or unsweetened American chocolate (with ½ teaspoon ground cinnamon and 4 teaspoons sugar added if American chocolate is used)
4 cups water

1. Bring 2 cups of water to a boil in a saucepan; add the chocolate and stir until it dissolves completely.
2. Add remaining 2 cups of water and bring to a boil again. Beat with a *molinillo* or wire whisk until frothy, or whirl in a blender or food processor.

Serves 4

CHAMPURRADO
CHOCOLATE *ATOLE*

This ancient Aztec corn drink is always called *champurrado* when made with chocolate. It is about as fattening and as rich as a chocolate malted.

6 cups whole milk
3 ounces Mexican chocolate (or unsweetened American chocolate), grated
1 cup Quaker *masa harina*
2 cups water
1 cinnamon stick

¼ cup (packed) dark brown sugar (or to taste) (use *piloncillo* if you have it)

1. Heat the milk and chocolate in a saucepan, stirring to dissolve the chocolate. When the chocolate is completely dissolved, remove from the heat and set aside to keep warm.
2. Mix the *masa harina* with the water in another saucepan; place over low heat, add the cinnamon stick, and cook until the mixture has thickened and the *masa* becomes translucent. Add the chocolate milk and sugar. Stir to dissolve the sugar and simmer for a few minutes. Remove the cinnamon stick and serve the *champurrado* hot in cups or mugs.

VARIATION: Stir in the grated zest of 1 orange (or dried tangerine peel ground in a blender or food processor) along with the *masa* and cinnamon.

Serves 8

ATOLE CON LECHE
PLAIN *ATOLE* (AND FRUIT-FLAVORED *ATOLES*)

Atole con Leche is the basic *atole* to which any flavoring you wish can be added. Unlike *champurrado*, it is made with white sugar.

3 cups water
1½ cups Quaker *masa harina*
1 cinnamon stick (2 inches) or seeds scraped from 1 vanilla bean
1 cup sugar (or to taste)
3 cups milk (or part milk and part cream for a richer *atole*)

1. Stir the *masa harina* into the water in a saucepan; add the cinnamon stick or vanilla and simmer gently over low heat, stirring, until the mixture thickens and the *masa* becomes translucent.
2. Remove from the heat and stir in sugar and milk. Return to the heat and bring to a simmer, stirring to dissolve the sugar. Remove the cinnamon stick. Serve hot in cups or mugs.

To make fruit-flavored atoles: With the sugar, add 1½ cups crushed, mashed, or puréed bananas, raspberries, blueberries, strawberries, blackberries, pineapple, pears, apples, guava, peaches, or cherries.

To make nut-flavored atoles: With the sugar, add ½ cup ground walnuts, pecans, hazelnuts, or blanched and ground almonds—plus 3 well-beaten eggs.

Serves 6–8

CAFÉ MEXICANO
MEXICAN COFFEE

Café de Olla (page 148) or 4 cups strong hot coffee
4 ounces Kahlúa
Sweetened whipped cream
Ground cinnamon

Pour the hot coffee into 4 mugs; add 1 ounce Kahlúa to each. Top with whipped cream; dust with cinnamon.

Serves 4

MARGARITA

1 lime wedge
Mound of salt
1 ounce tequila
½ ounce Triple Sec, Cointreau, or any orange-flavored liqueur
Juice of ½ lime

1. Moisten the edge of a martini glass with the lime wedge. Dip the rim of the glass in the salt to coat.
2. Stir the tequila, Triple Sec, and lime juice with ice. Strain into the salt-rimmed glass.

Serves 1

TEQUILA SUNRISE

1½ ounces tequila
4 ounces orange juice
¾ ounce grenadine

Pour the tequila and orange juice into a tall glass filled with ice cubes or crushed ice. Add the grenadine, and as it sinks, watch the sunrise.

Serves 1

SANGRITA
TOMATO-TEQUILA-CHILI COCKTAIL

2 pounds fresh, ripe tomatoes, peeled and seeded (or 2 cups chilled
    tomato juice)
Juice of 2 oranges
Juice of 2 limes
1 medium (or small) onion, chopped
Salt and freshly ground pepper to taste
½ teaspoon *chile pequin* or cayenne pepper (or 3 to 6 *chiles serranos en
    escabeche* with a little of the liquid) or to taste
4 ounces tequila
4 lime wedges

    1. Place all the ingredients (except the tequila and lime wedges) in a
blender or workbowl of a food processor fitted with the steel blade.Whirl
until smooth (if the workbowl is small, do it in batches). The tomato mixture should be quite *picante*.
    2. Chill the tomato mixture well and serve in small glasses with 1 ounce
of tequila *on the side* and a plate of lime wedges. The two liquids are drunk
alternately with, perhaps, a little suck of lime between sips.

Serves 4

SANGRÍA
REFRESHING WINE PUNCH

2 cups water or club soda
½ cup sugar
2 cups fresh orange juice
3 tablespoons fresh lime juice
1 bottle (750 ml) dry red wine
Slices of orange, fresh pineapple, peaches, and/or apples

    Fill a large pitcher one-third full of crushed ice or ice cubes. Add the
water, orange juice, lime juice, and wine. Stir until the sugar is completely
dissolved. Add the fruit slices and allow to macerate for 10 minutes. Serve
over ice cubes in tall glasses.

VARIATION: A more powerful sangría can be made by substituting 1 cup of
          brandy for 1 cup of water.

          For Sangría de Naranja (Orange Sangría), substitute ½ cup of Coin-
          treau, Triple Sec, or other orange liqueur for the lime juice.

Serves 4–6

SANGRÍA BLANCO
WHITE SANGRÍA

1 cup sugar
½ cup fresh lime juice
1 bottle (750 ml) sauterne
¼ cup Triple Sec or other orange liqueur
1 bottle (32 ounces) club soda
Orange slices

Fill a large pitcher one-third full of crushed ice or ice cubes. Add the sugar, lime juice, sauterne, and Triple Sec. Stir until the sugar is completely dissolved. Just before serving, add the club soda and orange slices. Serve over ice cubes in tall glasses.

Serves 4–6

ROMPOPE
MEXICAN EGGNOG

This is a very rich drink served as an after-dinner liqueur in tiny cordial glasses. Some Mexicans like the flavoring to be cinnamon rather than vanilla—and usually make that decision at the liquor store rather than at home, because *rompope* comes bottled in Mexico. Because it is rare to find *rompope* north of the border, we offer this recipe.

6 cups milk
2 cups sugar
1 vanilla bean or 1 cinnamon stick
16 egg yolks
2 cups light rum or brandy

1. In a large saucepan, bring the milk, sugar, and vanilla bean to a boil, stirring constantly. Boil at a slow roll for about 10 minutes, or until it has reduced by about one-third. Remove from the heat and cool slightly, stirring frequently to prevent a skin from forming.

2. Beat the egg yolks until thick and pour into the lukewarm milk mixture. Return to the heat and simmer until the mixture coats the back of a spoon. Remove from the heat again. Cool.

3. When the *rompope* is cool, stir in the rum. Beat with a wire whisk, electric beater, or, a few cups at a time, in a blender or food processor. Bottle; cap tightly and refrigerate. Serve after a day or two.

NOTE: Leftover *rompope* can be refrigerated almost indefinitely. It also makes a fine hostess gift.

VARIATION: For a thicker *rompope* (and even richer!) add ¼ cup finely ground almonds or cashews along with the eggs.

Makes 2 quarts

INDEX

157